MW01132787

OVERTHINKING & ANXIETY?
THINK AGAIN

5 PRACTICAL STEPS TO TRANSFORM NEGATIVE
THOUGHTS, RELIEVE STRESS, & REGAIN FOCUS
EVEN IF YOU ARE OVERWHELMED & SKEPTICAL
ABOUT FINDING INNER PEACE

DEAN MIDDLEBURGH

© Copyright 2024 - **All rights reserved.**

The content contained within this book may not be reproduced, duplicated or transmitted without direct written permission from the author or the publisher.

Under no circumstances will any blame or legal responsibility be held against the publisher, or author, for any damages, reparation, or monetary loss due to the information contained within this book, either directly or indirectly.

Legal Notice:

This book is copyright protected. It is only for personal use. You cannot amend, distribute, sell, use, quote or paraphrase any part, or the content within this book, without the consent of the author or publisher.

Disclaimer Notice:

Please note the information contained within this document is for educational and entertainment purposes only. All effort has been executed to present accurate, up to date, reliable, complete information. No warranties of any kind are declared or implied. Readers acknowledge that the author is not engaged in the rendering of legal, financial, medical or professional advice. The content within this book has been derived from various sources. Please consult a licensed professional before attempting any techniques outlined in this book.

By reading this document, the reader agrees that under no circumstances is the author responsible for any losses, direct or indirect, that are incurred as a result of the use of the information contained within this document, including, but not limited to, errors, omissions, or inaccuracies.

TABLE OF CONTENTS

TRIGGER WARNING

The content in this book addresses the topic of anxiety and overthinking. It includes discussions on overcoming mental challenges and finding inner peace. The information provided may be intense for individuals currently experiencing heightened emotional distress or those sensitive to discussions about mental health. Reader discretion is advised, and it is recommended to approach this material with self-awareness and the recognition of personal boundaries. If you feel triggered or overwhelmed, consider seeking support from a mental health professional. Prioritize your well-being and proceed with caution.

INTRODUCTION

We drink the poison our minds pour for us and wonder why we feel sick.

ATTICUS

How often do you find yourself caught in this chaotic ballroom, twirling in the arms of your own mental complexities? We live in an age where the constant hum of information and the cacophony of choices brew a potent potion that we willingly sip, oblivious to the fact that it's slowly poisoning our well-being.

Consider the story of Mark. He lived with strict parents who believed that children shouldn't have friends and, rather, should stay indoors. Consequently, Mark lacked genuine friendships during his childhood, relying solely on school and church acquaintances. Loneliness became a prominent aspect of his teenage years, which led to an acute attention to detail in his interactions. Engaging in conversations was not a source of enjoyment for Mark; instead, it triggered a cascade of overthinking. He meticulously analyzed people's reactions, facial expressions, and subtle cues during discussions. Mark's mind raced through countless scenarios of how a conversation could go wrong, leading to self-doubt and the fear of being perceived as bothersome or boring.

Building and sustaining friendships proved challenging for Mark, as he struggled to maintain connections for extended periods. When he did connect with someone, his mind would leap into fantasies about the potential depth of the relationship, whether as close friends or even romantically. Despite occasional fatigue and a desire to overcome this overthinking pattern, Mark found it difficult to break the cycle. He described feeling paralyzed by the constant need to analyze every detail rather than taking decisive action. This tendency resulted in missed opportunities, eroding his confidence in pursuing various endeavors. Just like Mark, many of us are going through the same situation.

In our quest for tranquility, we tend to face a relentless battle against anxiety. This struggle is not limited to the confines of our mental well-being; it infiltrates every aspect of our lives. From Mark's story, it becomes clear that overthinking is not a mere annoyance; it's a silent assassin of joy that lurks in the shadows of our minds. It can slowly chip away at the foundation of our lives, leaving us paralyzed with indecision and stuck in a sea of anxiety. We tend to have a strong desire to escape this destructive cycle, which is why we always yearn to reclaim control and restore balance to our lives.

Our minds, just like a crowded marketplace, are bustling with thoughts—some helpful, others not so much. It's the never-ending chatter that keeps us awake at night, second-guessing decisions, and wrestling with scenarios that may never come to pass.

The struggle against overthinking is real, and it takes a toll. Our mental wellness becomes a battleground, and anxiety, like an uninvited guest, overstays its welcome. This cycle of overthinking breeds more anxiety, which creates a loop that seems impossible to escape. We tend to yearn for a respite—a way to break free from the chains that bind our thoughts and, consequently, our lives.

It's not just about the mental toll; our physical health bears the burden too. Stress, a close companion of overthinking, finds its way into our bodies, affecting everything from our sleep to our immune systems. Overthinking—when left unchecked—becomes a silent saboteur that infiltrates every aspect of our lives.

As we navigate the maze of our thoughts, the impact extends beyond our own well-being. Our relationships, both personal and professional, bear witness to the ripple effect of anxiety. The people around us, like collateral damage, feel the aftershocks of our mental turmoil. Deep down, we want to change for the better because we know that it will not only liberate us but also enhance the quality of our connections.

Yet, seeking help remains a challenge. The financial burden and the societal stigma that are associated with mental health issues create a barrier, which leaves us struggling alone with our thoughts. But here's the good news: There's a way out, and it doesn't involve costly therapy sessions or unending prescriptions. The solution is in this book. Before anything, it is important to note that this book recognizes the toll overthinking has taken on your well-being, relationships, and opportunities for personal growth. It could be a missed opportunity due to indecision, the strain on relationships, or the sheer exhaustion of a mind in perpetual turmoil. With all these, this book emerges as your beacon of hope, offering you practical solutions that go beyond the conventional approaches that would allow you to regain control of your life.

Through this book, you will be introduced to the think AGAIN framework—a guide that will revolutionize the way you go about your thoughts. It is not about suppressing your mind but about rewiring it for resilience. This book is not a mere collection of platitudes; it is a guide providing you with actionable steps to redirect your thoughts and change your perspectives. By employing established methods rooted in neuro-linguistic programming (NLP), cognitive-behavioral therapy (CBT), and other inventive approaches, you can find comfort and break free from the constraints of excessive overthinking.

The benefits of undertaking this journey are numerous. This book promises shortcuts, offering you a faster route to breaking free from the chains of overthinking. Imagine having the power to make decisions without the paralysis of analysis, the ability to pursue opportunities without the burden of doubt, and the capacity to foster healthier relationships by conquering the anxiety that taints them.

Through this book, you will be able to utilize tried and tested techniques to suit your individual needs and incorporate practical habits to help you lead a more worry-free life for good. The result? A vivid picture of a better life unfolds—one where the mind is a tool, not a tormentor, and where clarity and confidence pave the way for success and fulfillment.

As you embark on this journey, you might wonder, "Why is the author the right guide for me?" The answer lies in my journey—a journey that mirrors the struggles of every over-thinker. Even though I am a trained sleep, stress, and recovery coach and an NLP practitioner, I am not an unapproachable guru. I had to learn how to traverse the perilous seas of overthinking before emerging with insight to give. I understand the difficulty of the journey because I've lived it. I am also aware of the associated frustration of trying various methods that fall short, the fatigue of battling an overactive mind, and the yearning for a solution that feels tailored to individual needs.

This book is a lifeline if you are drowning in a sea of over-thinking, tossed about by the waves of anxiety. So, get ready to think AGAIN and reclaim the peace and control that overthinking has stolen from you.

CHAPTER 1
RUMINATING ON YOUR RUMINATION

You are not going to worry yourself out of a problem.

ECKHART TOLLE

This quote emphasizes that relying on excessive worry to solve a problem is ineffective. It's especially true when the problem itself is the act of worrying or overthinking. In these situations, the more you obsess over the issue, the more you get trapped in a cycle, making the problem seem insurmountable. It is important to know that you need to move away from a mindset centered on perpetual worry. Instead, your focus should shift to practical solutions and positive perspectives. Constant worrying seldom leads to resolving issues; rather, it tends to amplify them.

OVERTHINKING

Overthinking is essentially what its name implies—it's the act of thinking excessively. It involves repeatedly going over the same thoughts and dissecting even the most straightforward situations or events to the point where any sense of proportion is lost. When you are caught in a cycle of overthinking, your mind tends to struggle to turn these thoughts into practical actions or positive outcomes. As a result, this mental process often leads to increased feelings of stress and anxiety.

Overthinking can affect anyone, and it affects them negatively. To better understand overthinking, let's say John has a job interview scheduled for the next day. Instead of preparing for the interview by focusing on his skills and qualifications, John starts overthinking. He begins to excessively dwell on possible negative scenarios, such as imagining he might forget important details, stumble over his words, or make a poor impression. John replays these thoughts repeatedly in his mind, analyzing every potential outcome until he becomes overwhelmed with anxiety. As a result, he finds it challenging to concentrate on the actual preparation for the interview and struggles to translate his concerns into constructive actions, ultimately creating unnecessary stress for himself.

Are you just worried or are you overthinking?

In simpler terms, overthinking is something we all do to some extent, especially when we care about our responsibilities and relationships. Whether it's as parents, children, employees, or businesspeople, worrying is often a sign of caring and wanting to do well.

However, there's a difference between regular worrying and overthinking. Regular worrying typically involves concerns about the future, like meeting deadlines or finding a suitable place for a family member. Worries can be productive in these cases as they help us plan and navigate challenges.

On the other hand, overthinking, or "ruminating," is when people get stuck replaying past events in their minds. It's a passive process that dwells on what has already happened, often blowing things out of proportion. For example, if someone accidentally calls their new boss by the wrong name, a regular worrier might feel a bit embarrassed but move on, maybe planning to apologize the next day. An overthinker, however, might obsessively replay the mistake, imagining various negative outcomes, like missing out on promotions or even getting laid off. The overthinking mind tends to create exaggerated scenarios, turning a small error into a major source of anxiety.

This tendency to dwell on the past and predict overly negative futures is a key characteristic of overthinking, and it can affect various aspects of a person's life. Even seemingly trivial events can trigger a cascade of exaggerated thoughts and worries in an overthinking mind.

Is It a Mental Illness?

No, overthinking itself is not officially recognized as a standalone mental health condition. Instead, it is commonly viewed as a symptom or trait connected to mental health conditions like depression or anxiety. In particular, over-thinking is often associated with Generalized Anxiety Disorder (GAD), which is characterized by excessive worry about various aspects of life.

GAD may have multiple causes, including genetic factors, specific life experiences, and personality traits that make it challenging to handle uncertainty. Typically, a combination of these factors contributes to the development of GAD.

Traits individuals with GAD tend to exhibit include:

- **Excessive Worry:** This involves persistent and heightened worry about multiple aspects of life that lasts for at least six months.
- **Difficulty Controlling Anxiety:** Challenges in managing and controlling anxiety can negatively impact daily functioning.
- **Physical Symptoms:** These may include restlessness, difficulties in concentration, and disruptions in sleep patterns.

In essence, while overthinking itself is not a diagnosed condition, it often serves as a noticeable feature in individuals dealing with generalized anxiety or other mental health challenges.

Overthinking and anxiety often go hand in hand like a duo in a comedy act, playing off each other's quirks and amplifying the chaos. Imagine overthinking as the overenthusiastic friend who never knows when to hit the brakes, constantly analyzing every possible scenario with the intensity of a detective solving a mystery. Meanwhile, anxiety is the jittery sidekick, nervously pacing in the background, fueled by the overthinker's relentless mental gymnastics.

The link between overthinking and anxiety is a self-reinforcing loop. Overthinking magnifies perceived threats, contributing to anxious thoughts. Consequently, anxiety intensifies these threats, which creates a negative thought loop. The constant worry fuels perpetual rumination, trapping the mind in endless concerns. This overactive thought process intensifies anxiety, creating a self-reinforcing pattern. It's akin to a tag team match where overthinking tags anxiety into the ring, forming an unbeatable duo of mental turmoil.

THE ROLE OF YOUR CHILDHOOD

Childhood experiences, like a wild mixtape of emotions and events, can lay the foundation for the epic saga of overthinking that unfolds in our adult lives. Traumatic experiences, awkward childhood moments, and the lessons we unwittingly absorb from our surroundings can all contribute to the overthinking symphony that plays on repeat in our heads.

Let's talk about the trauma pool first. Childhood traumas, whether big and splashy or subtle and insidious, leave a mark deeper than a catchy jingle you can't get out of your head. If you've been through the wringer during your formative years, the aftermath can manifest in a relentless cycle of overthinking. Picture it: As a kid, if something bad happens —maybe your parent's divorce, there's a loss of a loved one, or you're in an emotionally tumultuous environment—your young brain, still figuring out the ropes of the world, takes a hit. Instead of processing and moving on, your brain gets stuck in a loop, replaying the trauma like a broken record. Fast forward to adulthood, those ingrained patterns of over-analyzing and anticipating the worst become second nature.

Then there's the whole childhood-learning extravaganza. As kids, we're like sponges soaking up everything around us— the good, the bad, and the utterly bizarre. If you grew up in a household where every spilled glass of milk led to a Shake-spearean-level drama, you probably learned that the tiniest mishap was worth hours of fretting. It's like your brain got a crash course in Catastrophizing 101. So, as an adult, when your boss shoots you a stern look, your mind catapults into a catastrophic scenario of impending unemployment, bank-ruptcy, and a future living with your cat in a cardboard box all because you learned, back in the day, that small missteps equal big consequences.

Let's not forget those well-intentioned but slightly misguided nuggets of wisdom from caregivers. "Don't talk to strangers," they said. While it's solid advice for avoiding potential kidnappers, it inadvertently transformed into a mantra for overthinking social interactions. Now, as an adult, you find yourself dissecting every word and gesture in a conversation, even if it's just with the cashier at the grocery store. "Did I say something wrong? Did they think I was weird? Oh no, did I offend the person behind me in line by accidentally cutting in front?" Thanks, childhood rules— you've turned casual chit-chat into a mental gymnastics routine.

And let's not overlook the marvel that is comparison culture. Remember those school days when your friend aced the math test and, suddenly, you felt like the village idiot with a calculator? Childhood is the breeding ground for comparison, where your worth often gets measured against someone else's achievements. Fast forward to adulthood, and you're not just comparing grades; you're comparing relationships, careers, and the apparent success of others on social media. It's a recipe for overthinking deluxe—a constant mental tally of where you stand in the grand scheme of things.

IS THERE SOMETHING IN THE WATER?

Overthinking isn't just a quirk of an overactive mind; it's often a response to the environmental factors that surround us, which shape our thoughts and reactions. The world we live in, with its myriad complexities and challenges, can become a fertile ground for the seeds of overthinking to take root and flourish.

One significant environmental factor that can fuel overthinking is the incessant noise of the modern world. It's easy for our thoughts to become overloaded in this day of information overload when we're constantly exposed to a barrage of news, social media updates, and notifications. Our thoughts might become a disorganized symphony that won't stop due to the sheer amount of information and stimuli that bombard our minds. As we navigate this vast sea of data, our minds may struggle to filter out the irrelevant, resulting in a constant overanalysis of every piece of information.

The workplace, too, is pivotal in triggering overthinking. The competitive nature of many professional environments, coupled with tight deadlines and high expectations, can turn the mind into a pressure cooker. The fear of failure, the constant need to meet targets, and the anxiety about job security can brew a toxic concoction that feeds the over-thinking loop. The workplace, rather than being a space for creativity and productivity, can morph into a battleground where every decision and action is scrutinized within the recesses of our minds.

Family dynamics also contribute significantly to the environmental landscape of overthinking. The expectations and judgments, whether real or perceived, within familial relationships can create a breeding ground for self-doubt. The desire to live up to familial standards or the fear of falling short can spark a cascade of overthinking, turning simple interactions into complex mental puzzles.

Urban living, with its relentless pace and constant stimuli, can be a silent culprit in the overthinking saga. The hustle and bustle of city life, coupled with the sensory overload of traffic, crowds, and constant visual stimulation, can leave little room for mental peace. The absence of quiet spaces for contemplation can make it challenging to escape the over-thinking trap as the mind struggles to find moments of respite amid the urban chaos.

In the age of social media, the comparisons fostered by online platforms can act as a powerful catalyst for overthinking. The carefully curated depictions of others' lives, often showcasing the highlight reel rather than the full story, can trigger feelings of inadequacy and self-doubt. The temptation to compare our behind-the-scenes struggles with others' polished presentations can fuel a never-ending cycle of overthinking our own lives.

Even something as seemingly unrelated as weather can play a role in influencing our mental state. Gloomy, rainy days might cast a shadow on our mood, while scorching heat can lead to irritability and discomfort. These weather-induced shifts in mood can create an additional layer of complexity, adding to the environmental factors that contribute to over-thinking.

Crime levels in a particular area can have pronounced effects on individuals' mental health, with females often experiencing a heightened risk of depression and anxiety. The constant sense of insecurity and worry that comes with high crime rates might harm mental resilience.

Another environmental factor that might affect mental health is air pollution. Research indicates a correlation between increased rates of depression in more polluted areas. Long-term exposure to air pollution increases the risk of anxiety, and brief exposure raises the risk of suicide. This underscores the far-reaching consequences of environmental factors beyond their physical health implications.

The presence of toxins within one's home, such as those found in cleaning products and mold, also contributes to mental health issues. Mold exposure, in addition to causing physical health problems like asthma, can exasperate mental health challenges. The connection between environmental toxins and mental well-being emphasizes the importance of maintaining a healthy living space.

Poverty, with its complex web of social stress, stigma, and trauma, is a powerful environmental factor influencing mental health. Both children and adults living in poverty often face heightened mental health risks, leading to issues like depression and anxiety. The compounding effects of unemployment and strained relationships set up a difficult-to-break cycle that exacerbates mental health issues in underprivileged areas.

OVERTHINKING AS A TRAUMA RESPONSE

We often underestimate the toll overthinking and negative thought patterns take on our mental well-being, brushing them off as just quirks of our personality. However, diving a bit deeper, it becomes apparent that these habits may be more than just annoying traits—they can be subtle manifestations of trauma responses.

Imagine your brain as a well-intentioned security guard trying to protect you from potential threats. Now, trauma, be it big or small, is like an unexpected break-in that shatters the calmness of your mental security. Your brain, trying to make sense of the chaos, goes into overdrive, constantly scanning for danger. This heightened state of alertness is where overthinking steps in.

Trauma causes your brain to remodel itself to become hypervigilant about possible danger. It's like your mind becomes a detective on high alert, scrutinizing every situation for signs of danger. This hypervigilance often manifests as overthinking—a relentless loop of thoughts trying to anticipate and control every possible outcome. Your brain, in its attempt to keep you safe, ends up trapping you in a cycle of worry.

Negative thought patterns, on the other hand, are the pesky weeds that sprout from the fertile ground of trauma.

Imagine a garden where the seeds of negativity are planted during challenging times. If left unchecked, these seeds grow into a thicket that clouds the sunshine of positivity. Trauma can skew your perspective, making it difficult to see the brighter side of things. Negative thought patterns become a default setting, coloring your view of the world in shades of doubt and pessimism.

But why does your brain resort to these coping mechanisms? It's a survival instinct. When you've been through tough times, your brain becomes wired to expect the worst. It's like a self-defense mechanism, preparing you for potential threats. The problem arises when this defense mechanism becomes a constant state, leaving little room for joy and relaxation.

Overthinking and negative thought patterns can be so ingrained that they become a sort of armor, protecting you from disappointment and hurt. The downside is that this armor, while seemingly impenetrable, can be isolating. It keeps you guarded, preventing you from forming deep connections and fully experiencing life.

Meet Adam, a tough-as-nails veteran who has faced more battles than most people can fathom. His military career was a rollercoaster of adrenaline, camaraderie, and unimaginable challenges. However, the price he paid for his service was steep. In the field, he witnessed the horrors of war, losing friends, and facing the constant threat of danger. While he physically left the battlefield, the war continued in his mind.

Adam's overthinking is his brain's way of staying hyper-vigilant, always on the lookout for potential threats. Every unexpected noise triggers a flood of memories from his time in combat. The constant replay of these traumatic experiences in his mind makes it hard for him to relax, leading to a perpetual state of anxiety. Negative thought patterns become a protective shield, preparing him for the worst-case scenario. "What if something bad happens?" becomes a default setting—an echo from the war zone.

Similarly, let's meet Ashley, a vibrant soul whose life took an unexpected turn after a severe accident. The incident left her physically scarred and emotionally battered. Ashley found herself trapped in a web of overthinking and negativity as she grappled with the aftermath of her trauma. Simple tasks that were once second nature became paralyzing thoughts of potential harm.

For Ashley, overthinking becomes a way to regain control over an uncontrollable situation as her mind spirals in a loop of "What if" scenarios, trying to anticipate every possible danger. Negative thought patterns act as a shield against more pain. In her mind, expecting the worst seems like a way to prepare for it—a misguided attempt to protect herself from further harm.

In both Adam and Ashley's cases, overthinking and negative thought patterns are like scars on the inside, remnants of their struggles that linger long after the external wounds have healed. The brain, in its attempt to survive, clings to these patterns as a way to cope with the overwhelming emotions associated with trauma.

A LOOK INTO THE OVERTHINKER'S BRAIN

From an evolutionary perspective, our brains have developed a tendency to engage in overthinking as a way to address challenges and solve problems. Various brain chemicals—dopamine, adrenaline, serotonin, and cortisol—are important in starting and maintaining these recurring thought patterns.

Dopamine, often linked to reward and motivation, kicks off the overthinking loop by encouraging problem-solving. When we're actively trying to find solutions, adrenaline is released, providing an extra burst of energy that leaves us feeling pumped. As the loop progresses and potential solutions emerge, serotonin, known as the "feel-good hormone" and mood regulator, contributes to the process. However, if the loop fails to produce desired outcomes, serotonin is blocked, and cortisol—the stress hormone—is released. This triggers a stress response, leading to unhealthy rumination.

Overthinking can manifest in different forms, such as rumination about the past or anxiety about the future. Two key neural networks in the brain—the default mode network (DMN) and the direct experience network—are instrumental in regulating our experiences. The DMN becomes active when our attention drifts during routine tasks, engaging in activities like brooding, imagining, and planning. It tends to shift thoughts toward the past or future. On the other hand, the direct experience network is activated when we are fully present and mindful of our surroundings. For instance, feeling the water in the shower or the bristles of a toothbrush on your teeth are experiences rooted in the present.

With all these brain chemicals and neural networks at play, you are going to find yourself overthinking.

SIGNS YOU'RE AN OVERTHINKER

Overthinking is something we all do to some extent, but for some, it reaches a whole new level, becoming a real challenge. It's not just harmless mental chatter; it can be a full-blown mind marathon. Let's break down some symptoms of overthinking and see if you've ever found yourself caught in this thought loop.

Post-Conversation Overthinking

First off, if you find yourself replaying conversations in your head long after they've happened, you might be an overthinker. Did your words unintentionally sting? Did that joke come off wrong? These questions can haunt your mind for the entire day, turning a simple chat into an Olympic-level mental gymnastics routine.

Heightened Anxiety About Revelations

Then there's the peculiar case of heightened curiosity when someone utters those words, "I want to tell you something." Normal curiosity? Sure. Overthinking? Definitely. Your brain goes into overdrive, concocting all sorts of scenarios. Whether it's your teacher, your boss, or just a friend, you're suddenly Sherlock Holmes trying to deduce what they're about to reveal, and it's all you can think about.

Apologizing Excessively

Now, let's talk about the sorry spree. Do you find yourself apologizing even when it's not your fault? Congratulations, you might have overthinking tendencies. In an argument, instead of standing your ground, you might start thinking, "Maybe it is my fault. Maybe I hurt them." And before you know it, you're on a "Sorry World Tour," even when you're the one who deserves an apology.

Nocturnal Overthinking

Sleep is supposed to be a sanctuary, but for overthinkers, it's when the brain decides to throw a midnight carnival. When the clock strikes 12, the overthinking party begins, featuring thoughts from two years ago or pondering the meaning of life. It's like your brain waits for the world to be quiet before launching into a monologue of worries and irrelevant issues. Sleep cycle disruption? Oh, absolutely.

Imagining and Worrying About Worst-Case Scenarios

And here comes the grand finale—imagining worst-case scenarios. Picture this: You're thinking about your future, your career, your relationships but instead of daydreaming about success and happiness, your mind takes a dark turn. Suddenly, you're contemplating disastrous scenarios that have a one-in-a-billion chance of happening. Marriage troubles, accidents, you name it. It's like your brain is a block-buster movie director, but unfortunately, it's producing a horror film.

HOW OVERTHINKING AFFECTS YOUR LIFE

Overthinking has an impact on not just our mental health, but also our physical health and overall well-being.

Health

Overthinking directly affects your blood pressure, stealing away your peace of mind and bringing stress into your life, which can raise blood pressure. This will eventually increase the risk of heart problems such as strokes or heart attacks. The increased stress may also lead to bad habits like smoking and excessive alcohol intake, jeopardizing your general health.

Overthinking is a notorious culprit when it comes to sleep troubles. Despite your efforts, the constant stream of thoughts can keep you awake at night. If you find yourself caught in the loop of overthinking, achieving a restful night's sleep becomes challenging. The consequence? Grogginess, irritability, and fatigue the next day, making it difficult to focus on work, reducing productivity, and potentially contributing to weight gain through overeating.

Overthinking can play tricks on your appetite. Even a brief period of overthinking can disrupt normal hunger signals because the busy mind fails to communicate to the brain that it's time to eat. Dr. Gadkar explains that stress from overthinking may lead to either a loss of appetite or overeating, both of which can be detrimental to your overall health.

The impact of overthinking extends to the very structure and connectivity of your brain, potentially leading to mood disorders and mental health challenges such as anxiety, stress, and depression. This cognitive overload can diminish your ability to focus, affecting problem-solving skills and decision-making capabilities.

Overthinking takes a toll on your digestive system by inducing stress that reduces blood flow and oxygen supply to the stomach. The effects of stress on the body may result in gastrointestinal issues such as inflammatory bowel disease (IBD) or irritable bowel syndrome (IBS), causing disruptions to the regular operation of the digestive system.

The immune system takes the burden of overthinking-induced stress. Stress-induced cortisol production impairs the immune system, making you more prone to allergies, infections, and other disorders. Chronic stress caused by overthinking can impair the body's ability to defend itself against external dangers, putting overall health at risk.

Life

Physically, the impact should not be underestimated. Over-thinking induces stress, which releases cortisol, the body's stress hormone, leading to health issues like disrupted sleep, weakened immunity, and even weight gain. The physical toll includes headaches, muscle tension, and other stress-related ailments.

Chronic overthinking interrupts sleep, resulting in weari-ness and impaired cognitive performance because mental and physical health are inextricably linked. This impedes daily duties, decision-making, and healthy relationship maintenance. Persistent mental chatter reduces concentra-tion and productivity, impeding professional and personal development.

In the broader context of our lives, overthinking acts as a significant roadblock, fostering indecision and entangling the mind in potential outcomes and consequences. The lack of decisiveness results in overlooking potential opportunities, strained relationships, and a feeling of personal development stagnation. Overthinking contributes to a negative worldview, influencing perceptions and attitudes toward oneself and others.

Socially, overthinking has noteworthy implications. Constant preoccupation may lead to social withdrawal that is driven by fear of judgment or overanalysis of past interactions. This isolation worsens mental health issues and hinders interpersonal relationships.

INTERACTIVE ELEMENT

Overthinking Assessment Questionnaire

Instructions: For each question, select the response that best describes your thoughts and behaviors. Be honest in your responses to get an accurate assessment of your overthinking tendencies.

Scoring: Assign the following points to your responses:

- Rarely or Never: 1 point
- Occasionally: 2 points
- Often: 3 points
- Almost Always: 4 points

How frequently do you find yourself replaying past conversations or interactions in your mind?

- Rarely or Never
- Occasionally
- Often
- Almost Always

When faced with a decision, how likely are you to envision multiple potential outcomes and consequences?

- Rarely or Never
- Occasionally
- Often
- Almost Always

How often do you experience difficulty in falling asleep due to thoughts racing through your mind?

- Rarely or Never
- Occasionally
- Often
- Almost Always

When someone mentions wanting to talk to you, how anxious do you become about the possible reasons for the conversation?

- Rarely or Never
- Occasionally
- Often
- Almost Always

How frequently do you apologize, even when it's not your fault, because you believe you might have hurt someone with your words or actions?

- Rarely or Never
- Occasionally
- Often
- Almost Always

Do you often worry about future events, imagining worst-case scenarios that are unlikely to happen?

- Rarely or Never
- Occasionally
- Often
- Almost Always

How much time do you spend thinking about past mistakes or regrets?

- Rarely or Never
- Occasionally
- Often
- Almost Always

When faced with a challenge, how likely are you to doubt your abilities to overcome it?

- Rarely or Never
- Occasionally
- Often
- Almost Always

How often do you find yourself unable to enjoy the present moment because your mind is preoccupied with various thoughts?

- Rarely or Never
- Occasionally
- Often
- Almost Always

In social situations, how often do you feel the need to plan and rehearse what you will say beforehand?

- Rarely or Never
- Occasionally
- Often
- Almost Always

Scoring:

- 10–20 points: Low likelihood of overthinking
- 21–30 points: Moderate tendency for overthinking
- 31–40 points: High likelihood of overthinking
- 41–50 points: Very high likelihood of overthinking

Interpretation: The higher your score, the more likely you are to engage in overthinking behaviors. Consider seeking strategies to manage overthinking if your score indicates a significant tendency in this direction.

It is now time to empower you to reshape your internal monologue, embrace self-compassion, and banish perfectionism to build a mental fortress against self-doubt and negativity.

CHAPTER 2

A: ADJUSTING YOUR SELF-TALK

Don't believe everything you tell yourself.

LIDIA LONGORIO

You shouldn't unquestioningly accept every thought or belief that crosses your mind. Your internal narratives, thoughts, and self-talk may not always be accurate or beneficial. Instead of blindly trusting every thought that arises, critically examine your beliefs, question your assumptions, and be mindful of the potential influence of biases or negative patterns of thinking. In essence, it is important to be self-aware and have a more discerning approach to your own thoughts and internal dialogue.

OVERTHINKING AND SELF-ESTEEM

In our minds, overthinking and self-esteem twirl around each other like a couple unsure of who leads and who follows. It's a complicated tango, where one misstep can send the other spiraling, creating a perplexing chicken-and-egg relationship. Are you overthinking because your self-esteem is low, or is your self-esteem suffering because you can't stop overthinking? In our minds, where do thoughts and self-worth collide?

Imagine you're lying in bed, staring at the ceiling, replaying a conversation you had earlier in the day. Your mind dissects every word, every pause, and every raised eyebrow. This is overthinking in its purest form. It's as if your brain has become a relentless detective, searching for clues and hidden meanings that may not even exist. And what's the underlying soundtrack to this mental spectacle? A whispering voice questioning your every move and word. That, my friend, is your self-esteem playing a supporting role.

Overthinking often finds its roots in a shaky foundation of self-esteem. When you don't feel confident in yourself, your actions, or your decisions, your mind kicks into overdrive, trying to compensate for what it perceives as inadequacies. It's like a protective mechanism gone haywire, constantly on the lookout for potential pitfalls and dangers. So, in this sense, low self-esteem becomes the seed from which the overthinking weed grows.

But here's the catch—overthinking doesn't just stop at being a side effect of low self-esteem; it can also be the culprit behind the crumbling castle of self-worth. Just picture a moment when you're facing a dilemma, and instead of trusting your instincts, you start to overanalyze every possible outcome. You second-guess yourself, drowning in a sea of hypotheticals. The more you overthink, the more you question your abilities and judgment. And voilà There goes your self-esteem taking a nosedive.

The overthinking and self-esteem relationship is a cycle—a loop of doubt and analysis that feeds on itself. It's like a chicken and egg arguing about who came first, each influencing and reinforcing the existence of the other.

Consider another instance where a teenager anxiously stands before a mirror, picking apart every perceived flaw. Their acne, their hair, their clothes—nothing escapes scrutiny. That teenager is not just obsessing over their physical appearance; they're struggling with the tangled web of self-esteem and overthinking. The overthinking whispers, "What if people judge you for how you look?" and the self-esteem, already fragile, cowers under the weight of imagined judgements.

Now, let's shift the spotlight to the workplace. Let's say you submit a project, and suddenly, the seeds of doubt take root. Did you make a mistake? Could it have been better? The overthinking kicks in, and your self-esteem—already bruised from past experiences—starts to crumble. The fear of failure transforms into a self-fulfilling prophecy; the more doubt you harbor, the greater the likelihood of stumbling.

HOW TO TALK TO YOURSELF THE RIGHT WAY

Self-talk is essentially the ongoing conversation you have with yourself, often referred to as your inner voice. It's like a running commentary in your mind that blends your conscious thoughts with ingrained beliefs and biases, shaping an internal monologue that accompanies you throughout the day.

Most of the time, you might not even be consciously aware that this inner dialogue is happening, but rest assured, it's there. It's the narrator of your personal story, commenting on your experiences, decisions, and emotions.

How you talk to yourself is a powerful determinant of your self-doubt or self-confidence—it's like an internal compass guiding your beliefs and actions. Throughout your life, you'll engage in more conversations with yourself than with anyone else. That makes your self-talk incredibly significant. The words you choose in this internal dialogue contribute to shaping your self-image, influencing your behavior, and impacting your achievements.

Your self-talk operates in a continuous cycle, and it's crucial to be mindful of it. As Ralph Charell, an American author, aptly puts it, "The inner speech, your thoughts, can cause you to be rich or poor, loved or unloved, happy or unhappy, attractive or unattractive, powerful or weak (Bartwal, 2021)." This highlights the profound impact your self-talk can have on various aspects of your life.

Consider self-talk as the script you use to give form to your experiences. If this script is dominated by negative messages, your mind tends to internalize and reinforce them, shaping a thought process that leans toward pessimism. On the other hand, engaging in positive self-talk initiates a different conversation within yourself. It prompts you to perceive the world in a positive light, fostering a sense of optimism and boosting your overall well-being.

In essence, your self-talk is a potent tool that contributes significantly to your mental landscape. If you constantly feed your mind with negativity, it will likely reflect in your thoughts, actions, and ultimately, your life. But, if you choose positive affirmations and constructive self-talk, you pave the way for a more optimistic and fulfilling existence.

It's crucial to monitor your self-talk, being mindful of the tone and content of your internal dialogue. Try to actively challenge negative thoughts by substituting them with positive affirmations. This deliberate practice has the power to reshape your self-perception and, consequently, impact your behavior, aligning it with your goals and aspirations.

Now, why does the way you talk to yourself matter? It is important in a way that it wields a considerable influence on how you feel and, consequently, the actions you take. It's a bit like having a coach inside your head—it can either be your biggest cheerleader, motivating and supporting you, or it can be a relentless critic, eroding your confidence and self-esteem. The following are the general benefits of self-talk:

- **Confidence Boost:** Constructive self-talk raises confidence, sidelining doubts and enabling focused goal achievement. Overcoming shyness and low self-image are facilitated and are essential for success where confidence is a key factor.
- **Depression Defense:** In combatting depression, positive self-talk introduces optimism which shifts perspectives with empowering thoughts like "I can do it" or "I am capable." This mental pivot helps alleviate mood swings and physical symptoms of depression.

- **Stress Reduction:** Positive self-talk serves as a stress-management tool, fostering a calmer, less anxious state. By alleviating mental and physical burdens, it provides a valuable defense against stress-related issues.
- **Heart Health Guardian:** Research suggests that positive self-talk reduces the risk of heart problems by eliminating stress. A positive outlook on life, cultivated through self-talk, correlates with a lower mortality risk which protects the heart.
- **Performance Enhancement:** When fatigue threatens performance, self-talk becomes a motivational force. To prevent the temptation to quit, phrases like "I can do it" generate confidence, enabling task completion with a positive mindset.

It is always important to embrace positive self-talk as it is indispensable for personal and professional success. Whether gearing up for a presentation or pursuing personal goals, fostering a habit of positive self-dialogue ensures the right mindset. When your inner voice takes on a positive tone, it becomes a source of encouragement. It nudges you forward, reminds you of your strengths, and helps you navigate challenges with a can-do attitude. Positive self-talk acts as a motivational force, propelling you toward your goals and fostering a sense of self-assurance.

On the flip side, negative self-talk can be a formidable adversary. Negative self-talk isn't confined to your thoughts; it often triggers regrettable actions. Whether it prompts you to confront someone, quit a job impulsively, or distance yourself from loved ones, it can lead to destructive outcomes.

Despite its destructive nature, some find comfort or false purpose in negative self-talk, making it challenging to let go. What many overlook is that this internal dialogue steals from your present by tethering you to the past. It robs you of your happiness, diverting attention from the positive aspects of life. Negative self-talk acts like a trap, clouding your mind with fears, stress, anger, and frustration, preventing you from enjoying the present and hindering your potential for a better future. Despite everyone carrying their burdens, it's not the circumstances that dictate happiness but one's reactions and responses to life's challenges.

Our confidence erodes with negative self-talk, which sows seeds of doubt and fear. Imagine your inner voice as a constant stream of criticism, highlighting perceived shortcomings and dwelling on past mistakes. This type of self-talk can create a self-fulfilling prophecy, holding you back from taking risks or pursuing opportunities because you've convinced yourself you're not capable.

How to Flip the Script

Reducing self-talk can significantly impact self-doubt or confidence. Various strategies cater to different individuals, so experimenting with a few can help identify what works best.

- To cultivate a more positive mindset, begin by pinpointing areas of negativity in your life, whether it's work, your daily commute, or relationships. Begin with small steps, concentrating on a specific aspect for positive change.

- Regularly assess your thoughts throughout the day. If negativity dominates, consciously reframe toward a more positive perspective.
- Embrace humor, allowing yourself to smile or laugh, especially during tough moments. When you find humor in your everyday experiences, you are prone to experiencing decreased levels of stress.
- Prioritize a healthy lifestyle, working to incorporate 30 minutes of exercise most days you can break this up into shorter sessions if needed. A balanced diet and stress management techniques further contribute to your well-being.
- Surround yourself with positive, supportive individuals. Seek out those who offer constructive advice and encouragement, minimizing exposure to negative influences.
- Engage in positive self-talk. Apply the golden rule: Speak to yourself as kindly as you would to others. Confront negative thoughts by substituting them with positive affirmations and expressing gratitude for the positive aspects of your life.

Neutral Self-Talk

Neutral self-talk is a powerful tool for overthinkers because it provides a balanced and realistic perspective that can ease the burden of incessant thoughts. Instead of solely focusing on positive affirmations, neutral self-talk involves adopting a more objective and non-judgmental approach toward oneself and situations.

For example, when facing a challenge, an overthinker might typically engage in negative thoughts, anticipating failure. Neutral self-talk, however, would entail acknowledging potential outcomes without attaching judgment. Phrases like "I will do my best and learn from the experience, regardless of the outcome" allow for a more rational and less emotionally charged perspective.

This approach avoids the extreme highs and lows associated with positive or negative self-talk. As an overthinker, you can find comfort in the middle ground, acknowledging your abilities and limitations without magnifying them. It's about fostering self-awareness and self-acceptance without undue praise or criticism.

By embracing neutral self-talk, you can create a mental space that promotes a healthier mindset. It becomes a pragmatic and manageable way to navigate challenges, which leads to resilience and reduces the cognitive load associated with constant self-analysis.

Here are some examples of negative self-talk followed by ways you can make it positive:

Negative Self-Talk	Positive Self-Talk
I am not good enough.	*I am capable and constantly improving. I have unique qualities that make me valuable.*
I always mess things up.	*Mistakes happen, and I learn from them. I am resilient and can overcome challenges.*
I will never succeed.	*Success takes time and effort. I am making progress, and each step brings me closer to my goals.*
I am a failure.	*I am learning and evolving through life's lessons.*
I will never be as good as others.	*I have unique strengths and talents. I am on my own journey, and that's something to celebrate.*
I am not smart enough.	*I am intelligent and capable of learning. My potential is limitless, and I can acquire new knowledge.*
I don't deserve happiness.	*I deserve happiness and fulfillment. I am worthy of positive experiences and relationships.*
Nobody likes me.	*I am a likable person with valuable qualities. I attract positive connections and friendships.*

I always make the wrong decisions.	I use my knowledge and experiences to make well-informed decisions. I believe I will make the right decisions.
I am a burden to others.	I make a difference in the lives of people around me. My presence is valuable and appreciated.
I will never be happy.	I deserve to be happy, and I can achieve it. I have the power to design a happy and fulfilling life for myself.
I am not attractive.	*I am unique and attractive in my own way. True beauty comes from confidence and self-acceptance.*
I can't do it.	I'm capable of taking on and overcoming challenges. I have confidence in my abilities.
I will never get over this.	*I am resilient, and I have the strength to overcome difficulties. Time heals, and I will grow from this experience.*
I don't have anything to offer.	*I have valuable skills, talents, and perspectives to share. I contribute positively to the world around me.*

OVERCOMING PERFECTIONISM

In this current world that often demands excellence, the pursuit of perfection has become an ingrained part of many lives. While the pursuit of high standards can be admirable, the relentless pursuit of perfection can lead to a perilous path of overthinking and eventual despair. Perfectionism, characterized by an unattainable quest for flawlessness, not only hinders personal growth but also leads to a mindset that can be detrimental to your mental well-being.

Perfectionism and Overthinking

Chasing perfection is like trying to catch a butterfly with your bare hands—elusive and, honestly, a bit exhausting. The desire for flawlessness often morphs into overthinking, creating a mental maze that's hard to escape.

Perfectionism turns even the simplest tasks into an Olympic-level competition. It is not simply about achieving success; rather, it revolves around executing every task in an impeccably flawless manner. This constant need for excellence becomes a breeding ground for overthinking. Every decision and every move is dissected like a frog in a high school science class, and it's enough to make your head spin.

It's not just about personal standards either; societal expectations play a massive role. Social media has turned life into a highlight reel, making everyone's achievements look like a blockbuster movie. The pressure to measure up to these picture-perfect standards kicks your overthinking mind into overdrive. *Am I good enough? Am I doing it right?* It's a never-ending loop.

Then there's the fear of judgment—the silent killer of spontaneity. Perfectionists are often paralyzed by the what-ifs. *What if I mess up? What if people laugh at me?* These worries turn decision-making into a stressful game of mental chess, where every move is analyzed to avoid potential embarrassment.

Signs You're a Perfectionist

Perfectionists are similar to high achievers but with a few important variances. Here are the signs that you can use to tell if you are a perfectionist.

- **All-or-Nothing Thinking**

Imagine setting a goal for yourself, and it's like aiming for a bull's-eye every time. While high achievers might celebrate getting close to the target, for a perfectionist, it's all or nothing. Anything less than perfection feels like a failure, and there's no room for the "almost perfect" zone.

- **Being Highly Critical**

Perfectionists tend to be more critical, not just of themselves but also of others. High achievers appreciate their accomplishments and support others, but they often spot mistakes and imperfections, both in themselves and those around them.

- **Feeling Pushed by Fear**

A perfectionist's drive comes more from a fear of falling short rather than a genuine desire to achieve. High achievers are pulled toward their goals by passion; for perfectionists, it's the fear of not meeting a perfect standard that pushes them forward.

- **Having Unrealistic Standards**

Setting the bar too high is their trademark. While high achievers enjoy reaching their goals and then going a bit further, perfectionists tend to set goals that are initially out of reach, making it a constant struggle to meet those unrealistic standards.

- **Focusing Only on Results**

Perfectionists fixate on the end goal, often missing the joy in the journey. High achievers find fulfillment in the process, but for perfectionists, it's hitting that goal and avoiding any hint of failure that matters, making the journey less enjoyable.

- **Feeling Depressed by Unmet Goals**

When things don't go perfectly, they find it challenging to bounce back. Unlike high achievers who can move on from disappointments, perfectionists tend to beat themselves up, dwelling on negative feelings when their high expectations aren't met.

- **Fear of Failure**

Failure is a daunting prospect. Since anything less than perfection feels like a failure, this fear can make it difficult to start something new. It's the anxiety of not meeting that impeccable standard that often holds perfectionists back.

- **Procrastination**

Paradoxically, their fear of imperfection can lead to procrastination. The worry about doing something less than perfect can paralyze perfectionists, leaving tasks unfinished and contributing to a cycle of self-doubt.

- **Defensiveness**

Constructive criticism hits differently here instead of seeing it as a tool for improvement, perfectionists might react defensively, shielding themselves from the perceived pain of not being perfect.

- **Low Self-Esteem**

Striving for perfection doesn't always translate to high self-esteem for perfectionists. Constantly evaluating themselves critically and tending to push others away can lead to feelings of loneliness and lower self-esteem, impacting their overall satisfaction with life and relationships.

How to Overcome Perfectionism

So, how do you escape this perfectionist prison and the overthinking that comes with it? Here are some ways you can do that:

- **Become More Aware of Your Tendencies**

Take a moment to reflect on how perfectionism shapes your thoughts and actions. Write down these thoughts to gain a clearer understanding. By acknowledging how perfectionism influences your life, you can start changing your self-talk and approach.

- **Focus on the Positives**

Perfectionists often dwell on the negatives. Challenge yourself to identify three positive aspects for every one thing you're dissatisfied with. Recognizing the good alongside the perceived flaws helps create a more balanced perspective.

- **Allow Yourself to Make Mistakes**

Embrace the idea that mistakes are part of the learning process. Engage in activities where you're not expected to excel immediately. Focus on enjoying the journey and gradually improving. Mistakes are valuable growth opportunities.

- **Set More Reasonable Goals**

Perfectionists often set unattainable goals due to unrealistic standards. Set SMART goals, ensuring they are specific, measurable, attainable, realistic, and time-bound. Realistic and challenging goals reduce stress and boost confidence.

- **Learn How to Receive Criticism**

Perfectionists may take criticism personally, affecting self-esteem, so it is important to acknowledge that constructive feedback is crucial for your personal growth and development. Separate feedback from your self-worth and see it as a tool for improvement.

- **Lower the Pressure You Put on Yourself**

Acknowledge that the harshest critic is often yourself. Practice self-kindness by accepting that perfection is unattainable. If you're giving your best effort, that's commendable. Strive for excellence rather than perfection.

- **Focus on Meaning Over Perfection**

Shift your focus from perfection to finding meaning in your endeavors. If an activity brings joy and purpose, the pursuit of perfection becomes less significant. Fulfillment lies in the journey and the meaning it brings.

- **Try Not to Procrastinate**

Perfectionists often procrastinate to avoid imperfection. Overcome this by starting early, even if it's just an initial rough outline. Understand that perfection isn't achieved on the first attempt, and allow yourself the grace to refine your work over time.

- **Cut Negative Influences**

Be mindful of how external factors, like social media, reinforce perfectionism. Limit or eliminate exposure to channels promoting unrealistic standards. Protect your mental well-being by distancing yourself from negative influences.

- **Go to Therapy**

If perfectionism causes significant anxiety, consider therapy, particularly cognitive-behavioral therapy (CBT). Therapy helps reframe perfectionist thoughts and offers tools to understand the deeper reasons behind the pressure for perfection. Obtaining assistance from professionals offers further reinforcement in overcoming perfectionism.

BECOMING YOUR OWN CHEERLEADER

Self-Scripting

Self-scripting is a powerful technique that involves consciously shaping and directing your internal dialogue or "self-talk" to promote positive thinking, challenge unhelpful thoughts, and ultimately enhance your mental well-being. It's like being the author of your own story by actively creating a narrative that fosters a more positive and constructive mindset.

To practice self-scripting effectively, you can employ various methods of challenge to confront and reshape your unhelpful thoughts. Think of it as developing a persuasive argument where observable, concrete, and data-based examples serve as supporting evidence to strengthen your case against negative thinking. Here are some general tips and questions to guide you through the process:

1. Consider Different Perspectives

- How would someone I admire approach this situation?
- What might my classmates or friends think in this scenario?
- How would an impartial observer perceive the situation?

2. Reality Check

- What evidence aligns or opposes with my idea?
- How likely is it that my prediction will come true?
- Am I basing my belief on facts or assumptions?
- What has happened in similar situations before?

3. Check for Helpful Thoughts

- What's the most extreme situation I could encounter, and is it genuinely as bad as it seems?
- Will this matter in the long run, or is it a temporary concern?
- Is my thought genuinely helpful in this situation?
- Can I identify positive outcomes or alternative perspectives?

4. Explore Positive Alternatives

- What would be a more helpful and constructive thought?
- How would my friends view this situation in a positive light?

- Are there potential positive aspects or outcomes to consider?

5. Avoid Jumping to Conclusions

- Am I making predictions about the future without an adequate basis of evidence?
- Is there another way to interpret the situation?
- Do I need more information before forming a belief?

By consistently challenging your thoughts using these techniques, you can gradually shift your self-talk toward a more positive and realistic perspective. Self-scripting is a dynamic tool that empowers you to take control of your narrative, fostering personal growth and resilience.

How to Boost Your Confidence and Improve Your Self-Esteem

Confidence and self-esteem are the cornerstones of a fulfilling and successful life. Building and maintaining these qualities is an ongoing process that requires self-reflection, self-compassion, and intentional actions. Here are some powerful strategies to boost your confidence and enhance your self-esteem.

- **Recognize Your Strengths**

Firstly, recognizing what you're good at can be a powerful confidence booster. Whether it's a hobby, skill, or quality, identifying and appreciating your strengths can uplift your mood. Reflect on your talents and engage in journaling about activities that bring you a sense of accomplishment.

- **Build Positive Relationships**

Building positive relationships is equally crucial. Evaluate the impact certain people have on your self-esteem. If some bring you down, consider spending less time with them and actively seek relationships with positive individuals who appreciate and support you. Consider the reasons behind their positive impact on your life.

- **Practice Self-Kindness**

Being kind to yourself involves changing self-critical thoughts. Imagine advising a friend in a similar situation, then apply that kindness to yourself. Journal about moments of self-kindness and the positive outcomes they bring.

- **Learn Assertiveness**

Learning to be assertive is a key aspect of fostering self-esteem. Observe assertive individuals and emulate their communication style. Reflect on how being more assertive can positively impact your interactions and relationships.

- **Set Boundaries**

Saying "no" is a liberating skill, especially for those with low self-esteem who tend to overcommit. Reflect on instances where saying "no" could have benefited you, and practice gentle but firm ways to decline requests.

- **Accept Challenges**

Challenging yourself is a potent way to boost self-esteem. Set realistic goals and track your progress. Journal about the fears and doubts you experience, and celebrate your achievements, no matter how small.

Reflection Questions

1. What activities or skills do I excel at, and how do they make me feel?
2. Who are the people in my life that lift me up, and why?
3. How can I show more kindness to myself in moments of self-criticism?
4. Who do I admire for their assertiveness, and what specific behaviors can I incorporate into my own communication style?
5. In what areas of my life do I struggle to say "no," and how does it affect my well-being?
6. What goals can I set for myself to challenge and expand my comfort zone? How will achieving these goals impact my self-esteem?

INTERACTIVE ELEMENT: TAMING YOUR INNER CRITIC

Embark on a journey of self-discovery through the powerful NLP technique known as reframing. This engaging process aims to help you silence your inner critic and unravel the intricacies of negative self-perception and pessimism.

Reframing operates on the notion that altering your perspective on a situation can change how it affects you emotionally. It's about consciously shifting from a negative viewpoint to a positive one, essentially reshaping your mental landscape. Based on neuro-linguistic programming (NLP), reframing employs the language of the mind to reshape thought patterns.

To initiate reframing:

1. Recognize and challenge negative thoughts.
2. Analyze their validity and consider alternative, more constructive interpretations.
3. Break the cycle of self-criticism by replacing harsh inner dialogues with compassionate and encouraging language.

By reframing, you are working to empower yourself to view challenges as opportunities for growth, fostering resilience and optimism.

In conclusion, understanding the relationship between over-thinking and self-esteem is essential for mental well-being. By exploring self-talk, overcoming perfectionism, and becoming your own cheerleader, you can break the cycle of distorted thinking, which leads to resilience for a brighter outlook. Also, reframing techniques offer a practical tool for combating negative thoughts. For a comprehensive guide, refer to the provided resources. The upcoming chapter focuses on understanding and confronting distorted thinking patterns. The goal is to empower you to break the cycle and cultivate a brighter, more resilient mental outlook.

CHAPTER 3

G: GETTING RID OF ANTS

Sometimes, when things are falling apart, they may actually be falling into place.

J. LYNN

I n times of upheaval and chaos, apparent disarray may be a necessary prelude to positive change. You should understand that what may seem like a breakdown could be a transformative process, aligning pieces for a better future. Embracing uncertainty and trusting the unfolding journey may reveal unexpected opportunities and growth amid the perceived chaos.

WHY HUMANS ARE HARDWIRED FOR NEGATIVITY

Ever wondered why insults linger in our minds for ages, while compliments often fade away quickly? Well, it turns out our brains have a built-in "negativity bias." This means our brains are naturally more sensitive to bad news or negative experiences, and this bias can be traced back to the earliest stages of information processing.

Studies conducted by John Cacioppo have demonstrated that our brains exhibit a heightened response to negative stimuli. In his studies, when people were exposed to images evoking positive, negative, or neutral feelings, the brain exhibited a greater surge in electrical activity in response to negative stimuli. Essentially, our brains are hardwired to give more weight to negative information, a trait likely evolved to help us avoid danger and ensure survival.

This negativity bias isn't limited to insults; it extends to various aspects of our lives. In relationships, for instance, the ideal balance between negativity and positivity is crucial. Research indicates that a healthy marriage requires a 5:1 ratio of positive to negative interactions. Couples who maintain this balance, even if they argue frequently, tend to stay together and remain satisfied.

The significance of the 5:1 ratio is not limited to marriages; it holds true in other areas of life. It's the frequency of small positive acts that matters most. Occasional grand gestures might be enjoyable, but they don't counterbalance the brain's predisposition toward negativity. It takes consistent, small, and positive experiences—that occur five times more often than negative ones—to tip the scales toward happiness.

AUTOMATIC NEGATIVE THOUGHTS (ANTS)

ANTs are spontaneous and involuntary thoughts that tend to be negative and unhelpful, impacting our mood, behavior, and overall well-being. These thoughts often occur automatically without conscious effort and can shape our perceptions of ourselves, others, and the world around us.

ANTs or cognitive distortions often lead us down the rabbit hole of negativity, distorting our perceptions and influencing our emotions. Below are various automatic negative thoughts or cognitive distortions.

- **All-or-Nothing Thinking (Black-and-White Thinking)**

When you engage in all-or-nothing thinking, you often magnify small setbacks into catastrophic failures. This mindset neglects the nuances and shades of gray in life, pushing individuals to view situations as either entirely positive or entirely negative.

Imagine you're working on a project where things don't go exactly as planned. If you catch yourself thinking, "I totally messed up this project is a disaster," you might be engaging in all-or-nothing thinking. It's like viewing life through a pair of extreme-tinted glasses, ignoring the shades of gray. Life rarely fits neatly into "all good" or "all bad" categories.

This type of thinking involves seeing things in black and white terms without recognizing shades of gray. Overthinkers may struggle to see a middle ground and may perceive situations as either perfect or a complete failure.

- **Catastrophizing (Magnification or Minimization)**

Catastrophizing tends to amplify the significance of minor mishaps, projecting them onto the grand stage of life. Imagine this scenario: You spill coffee on your shirt before an important meeting. Catastrophizing kicks in when you start imagining your day unraveling like a tragic comedy: "Everyone will notice, the boss will think I'm incompetent, and my career is over!" Catastrophizing involves blowing things out of proportion. Instead of making a molehill out of a coffee stain, remember that people have short memories, and your career isn't hanging by a thread.

This involves imagining the worst-case scenario and expecting it to happen. People who engage in catastrophizing may blow things out of proportion, leading to increased anxiety and worry.

- **Overgeneralization**

Meet the fortune teller in your head—overgeneralization. If one bad thing happens, like a rejection from a job interview, you might think, "I always mess up interviews. I'm a failure." Overgeneralization occurs when broad conclusions are drawn from a single incident, and this tendency to generalize from limited evidence can contribute to overthinking. For example, if one negative event occurs, an overthinker may generalize it to believe that negative events will always happen.

This tendency to generalize negative experiences can result in overthinking as you begin to believe that a single failure defines your entire identity or professional journey. Recognizing that one setback doesn't dictate overall success can help break the cycle of overgeneralization and promote a more balanced outlook. In reality, one rejection doesn't define your entire professional journey. Don't let a single rainstorm convince you that life is a perpetual monsoon.

- **Filtering (Selective Abstraction)**

Filtering, also known as selective abstraction, involves narrowing one's attention to negative aspects while overlooking positive elements. Imagine you bake a batch of cookies, and everyone raves about their chewy deliciousness, except for one person who mentions they're a bit too sweet. If you filter, you will focus solely on the negative comment, ignoring the sea of compliments. It's like wearing negativity blinders, narrowing your perspective to only see the bad stuff. Remember, you can't please everyone, and a sprinkle of criticism doesn't spoil the whole batch.

Overthinkers may solely concentrate on the negatives in a situation, overlooking any positives, leading to a distorted and heightened sense of concern.

- **Mind Reading**

Imagine you're at a social gathering and someone glances your way. If your mind jumps to, "They must think I'm boring or awkward," congratulations, you're a mind reader! In reality, you can't pluck thoughts from someone's head. Assuming you know what others are thinking often leads to unnecessary anxiety and self-doubt. Instead, consider that people are often preoccupied with their own thoughts and might not be judging you as much as you think.

- **"Should" Statements**

"Should" is a demanding word, and when it dominates your thoughts, you might find yourself drowning in guilt. For example, "I should be more successful by now," or "I should always be happy." "Should" statements set unrealistic expectations, leading to disappointment. Swap out "should" for "prefer," and cut yourself some slack. Life's more enjoyable without the heavy burden of self-imposed "shoulds."

Overthinkers may impose rigid and unrealistic expectations on themselves, leading to feelings of guilt and inadequacy if they don't meet these standards.

- **Jumping to Conclusions**

Take this example: You're in a group chat, and it goes silent for a minute. If you jump to conclusions, your mind screams, "They must be mad at me!" Reality check: People have lives, and not every pause in communication is a sign of your impending social doom. Jumping to conclusions is like predicting a storm just because a breeze paused for a coffee break.

- **Discounting the Positive**

Imagine you aced a test, but your brain goes, "Oh, it was easy. Anyone could have done it." Discounting the positive is like being your own hype deflator. Instead of celebrating victories, you brush them off as flukes or luck. Newsflash: You're allowed to acknowledge and enjoy your wins. It's not bragging; it's self-love.

- **Personalization**

Imagine your friend cancels plans, and your mind instantly whispers, "It's because I'm boring." Personalization is like starring in a soap opera where everything revolves around you, even when it doesn't. Reality check: People cancel plans for a zillion reasons, most of which have nothing to do with your perceived entertainment value. Don't let your mind cast you as the lead in a melodrama that isn't yours.

Personalization involves taking responsibility for events that are beyond your control or assuming that everything is about yourself. Overthinkers may tend to attribute events to their own actions, even when there is no supporting evidence.

HOW TO GET RID OF ANTS

These distorted thoughts often arise spontaneously, coloring our perception of ourselves, others, and the world around us. Fortunately, challenging and dismantling these cognitive distortions is a crucial step toward fostering a more positive and realistic mindset. Here are the practical strategies we can employ to challenge and overcome these ANTs.

CBT Techniques

Cognitive Behavioral Therapy (CBT) is a powerful and widely practiced approach. Within CBT, various techniques are employed to help us navigate the different forms of our thoughts and emotions. Here are the different techniques we can employ.

Socratic Questioning

Imagine a teacher not providing answers but instead guiding you through a labyrinth of your own thoughts with questions. That's the essence of Socratic questioning in a nutshell. It's not about handing out solutions but rather about encouraging deep contemplation and self-discovery.

In the context of psychotherapy, Socratic questioning becomes a potent tool. Therapists utilizing this technique aim to dissect the foundations of their client's beliefs. It's a journey of exploration where the therapist, fueled by genuine curiosity, nudges the client toward examining the evidence and logic behind their thoughts. This process becomes a powerful ally in identifying and challenging irrational or harmful beliefs.

Now, think of it as a flashlight in the dark corners of the mind. Socratic questioning sheds light on the murky waters of your assumptions and perceptions. It's a bit like therapy inception—getting therapy within therapy. While it's a technique rooted in CBT, its adaptability makes it a valuable asset across various therapeutic approaches.

Gathering Evidence

Alright, let's shift gears and don the detective hat. In the CBT toolbox, gathering evidence is just like collecting clues to solve the mystery of one's thoughts. Imagine your mind as a crime scene, and those unhelpful thoughts are the suspects. Instead of jumping to conclusions, CBT encourages individuals to gather evidence.

It's not about cherry-picking instances that confirm existing beliefs; it's about an unbiased investigation. You're looking for all the evidence: the good, the bad, and the indifferent. This process often unveils patterns in thinking that help us to step back and see the bigger picture.

Consider it as creating a mental crime board. Pinning up thoughts, emotions, and situations, and connecting the dots to see the larger narrative. It's a methodical approach that adds a layer of objectivity to the subjective realm of thoughts and feelings.

Cost-Benefit Analysis

This is like your mental balance sheet. In the financial world, a cost-benefit analysis helps in decision-making. Similarly, CBT is about evaluating mental investments and returns. Let's break it down without going into economic jargon.

Picture your thoughts as assets and liabilities. Now, imagine assigning values to these mental assets and liabilities. What impact do they have on your emotional well-being? The cost-benefit analysis in CBT aims to make these evaluations explicit.

It's a bit like auditing your mental portfolio. What thoughts contribute positively to your mental health, and which ones are dragging you down? By considering the costs and benefits, you can make informed choices about which thoughts to keep and which ones to let go of.

Thought Reframing

Ever wished you could mold your thoughts like clay? Well, thought reframing in CBT is pretty close to that. It's the art of reshaping perspectives, taking a negative thought and turning it into a more balanced or positive one.

Think of it as a mental renovation project where you identify a thought that's causing distress, deconstruct it, and then rebuild it with a more constructive mindset. It's not about sugarcoating reality but rather seeing it from a different angle.

It's like having a pair of thought glasses that let you see the same situation with a different tint. By altering the way you perceive events, thought reframing becomes a powerful tool in promoting resilience and reducing unnecessary stress.

Positive Affirmations

Take positive affirmations as little notes of encouragement you leave for yourself on the mirror every morning. In the world of CBT, positive affirmations are like pep talks for the soul.

They're short, powerful statements aimed at promoting a positive mindset. While some might dismiss them as mere feel-good mantras, there's a psychological underpinning to their effectiveness. Through consistently affirming positive beliefs, individuals can rewire their brains, nurturing a more optimistic perspective.

It's like planting seeds of positivity in the garden of your mind. The more you water them with affirmations, the more likely they are to bloom into a mindset that's resilient in the face of challenges.

How to Write Affirmations

Creating personal affirmations is a potent method for nurturing a positive mindset tailored to you. Affirmations are constructive statements you repeat to strengthen specific beliefs or mindsets. Use this guide to create your affirmations:

1. Identify Areas for Improvement

Start by reflecting on areas of your life where you'd like to see positive change. Whether it's self-confidence, stress management, or goal achievement, pinpoint specific aspects you want to address. Being specific helps tailor your affirmations to your unique needs.

2. Be Positive and Present

Compose your affirmations in the present tense using positive language. Rather than phrasing them as future objectives, articulate them as if they are currently unfolding. This approach aids your subconscious mind in embracing and internalizing these positive statements.

3. Be Precise and Specific

Affirmations are most effective when they are concise and focused. Aim for clarity and specificity in your statements. Avoid vague or overly general affirmations; the more precise you are, the better your mind can grasp and work toward the goal.

4. Use Empowering Language

Choose words that evoke a sense of strength, determination, and empowerment. Opt for words that resonate with you. If certain words hold significant meaning or have a positive emotional charge, incorporate them into your affirmations.

5. Frame Affirmations Positively

Instead of stating what you don't want, frame your affirmations in a positive light. Focus on what you aspire to achieve or embody rather than what you want to avoid. Positive framing encourages a more optimistic and constructive mindset.

6. Make Them Believable

While affirmations are about cultivating a positive mindset, you must believe in what you're saying. If your affirmations feel too far-fetched or unrealistic, your mind might resist them. Ensure that your statements are within the realm of possibility and align with your values.

7. Personalize Your Affirmations

Tailor your affirmations to your unique experiences, strengths, and challenges. Personalization enhances their relevance and makes them more meaningful to you. Consider incorporating specific details about your life to make the affirmations deeply connected to your reality.

8. Repeat and Reinforce

Repetition is key to the effectiveness of affirmations, so consistently repeat your affirmations, preferably multiple times daily. Whether you say them aloud, write them down, or create visual reminders, the goal is to reinforce these positive statements consistently.

9. Use Visualization

Integrate visualization with your affirmations. As you affirm positive statements, visualize yourself embodying the qualities or reaching the goals mentioned. Visualization amplifies the impact of affirmations by vividly depicting success in your mind.

10. Update as Needed

As your goals and circumstances evolve, revisit and update your affirmations. Life is dynamic, and your affirmations should reflect your current aspirations. Regularly assess your progress and adjust your affirmations accordingly.

Examples of Personalized Affirmations:

1. My career path is filled with success, and I approach it confidently and competently.
2. Challenges are stepping stones to growth and wisdom, and I embrace them eagerly.
3. Setbacks only make me stronger, and I glean lessons from every experience.
4. I rely on my instincts and prioritize decisions that improve my well-being.
5. Each day, I evolve into a better version of myself, filled with potential.
6. Love and support surround me, and positivity gravitates toward me effortlessly.
7. I cherish my past, eagerly anticipate my future, and find contentment in the present.
8. I maintain control over my thoughts, fostering a mindset of positivity and hope.
9. I express gratitude for both big and small achievements, recognizing their significance.
10. I am worthy of love, respect, and all the joys life offers, and I welcome them with open arms.

Keep in mind that the power of affirmations hinges on your belief and dedication to them. Embrace the process, practice patience with yourself, and take joy in celebrating the positive changes as they gradually unfold.

CBT, with its arsenal of techniques, empowers us to become active participants in our mental well-being. It's not about erasing all negativity but about navigating through it with a compass of reason and a backpack of resilience. So, the next time the twists and turns of your thoughts seem overwhelming, remember, you've got a toolkit at your disposal—a toolkit designed not to fix but to empower.

Cultivating a Growth Mindset

A growth mindset is like having a mental superhero cape that whispers in your ear, "You can do it!" In simpler terms, it's the belief that your abilities, intelligence, and talents can be developed through dedication, hard work, and learning. Those who have a growth mentality view obstacles as opportunities for both professional and personal progress rather than as obstacles.

According to Professor Carol Dweck (2006):

> This growth mindset is based on the belief that your basic qualities are things you can cultivate through your efforts. Although people may differ in every way —in their initial talents and aptitudes, interests, or temperaments—everyone can change and grow through application and experience.

Growth Versus Fixed Mindset

In simple terms, having a growth mindset means seeing your abilities and intelligence as something you can develop and enhance over time through effort and learning. On the flip side, a fixed mindset is the belief that these traits are set in stone and unchangeable—you're stuck with whatever you've got.

Let's take the example of an aspiring entrepreneur who needs to understand basic finance skills for their business. If they have a fixed mindset, they might throw in the towel before even trying, thinking, "I've never been good at math or financial stuff. Running a business is not for me."

Now, switch gears to a growth mindset. In this scenario, the entrepreneur acknowledges their lack of financial background but chooses to see it as an opportunity to learn and improve. Their mindset shifts to, "I may not know much about finance now, but I can learn and practice until I become proficient."

Individuals who embrace a growth mindset view challenges as opportunities for learning and personal development. So, for our entrepreneurial friend, every financial hiccup or budgeting challenge becomes an opportunity to acquire new knowledge and skills.

A growth mindset is like a secret weapon in the world of entrepreneurship, where each day offers a new set of challenges. It is the concept that even if you do not already possess all of the necessary skills, you can acquire them through dedication and hard work. Instead of becoming obstacles, challenges become stepping stones, and each setback serves as a learning opportunity.

So, if you're building a business and find yourself in uncharted territory, a growth mindset becomes your guiding compass. It's the confidence that you can gather the necessary knowledge and skills along the way. While fixed-mindset folks might shy away from challenges, growth-mindset individuals embrace them as opportunities to evolve and thrive.

In a nutshell, whether you're crunching numbers for your business or tackling any entrepreneurial challenge, your mindset plays a crucial role. Embracing a growth mindset unlocks opportunities, ignites determination, and transforms every obstacle into an opportunity for learning and personal development. It's not just a mindset; it's a game-changer for those aspiring to succeed in the dynamic world of entrepreneurship.

You may still have this question: How can a growth mindset help combat negative thoughts or bias?

Remember that a growth mindset is your trusty shield against the arrows of negative thoughts and biases. When negative thoughts creep in, a person with a growth mindset doesn't accept them as absolute truths but instead questions and challenges them. It's like having a mental bouncer at the door, filtering out destructive thoughts. A growth mindset deconstructs the basis for negative thoughts by redefining challenges as opportunities for learning and growth. Moreover, it encourages individuals to examine their biases, fostering a more open and inclusive perspective.

How to Develop a Growth Mindset:

It's important to recognize that developing a growth mindset is a continuous journey, not a final destination. To begin, embrace challenges rather than evade them. Recognize that setbacks should be viewed not as failures but as stepping stones toward improvement. Shift your focus from seeking validation to seeking opportunities for learning and development. Embrace the power of "not yet"—if you don't know or can't do something now, it's not a permanent state; you just haven't reached that point yet.

Furthermore, rather than taking criticism as a personal attack, view it as helpful feedback. Recognize that criticism is a tool for improvement rather than an assessment of your skills. Surround yourself with people who have a growth mindset; their optimism and perseverance can be contagious. Never forget that learning and development are continuous processes; thus, it's acceptable to not know everything right away.

Helpful Tips:

- Consider your feelings and thoughts regularly. Awareness marks the initial stride toward change.
- Incorporate positive affirmations into your daily routine. Remind yourself that obstacles present chances and failures are only temporary.
- Instead of being obsessed with the end goal, concentrate on the process of learning. Celebrate your progress' tiny successes and turning points.
- Actively seek feedback from others by recognizing that constructive criticism is an important tool for personal growth.
- Adopt a mindset of continuous learning. Explore new interests, acquire new skills, and remain curious about the world around you.

In essence, a growth mindset is a transformative approach to life. It not only shields you from the negative but also propels you forward by turning challenges into catalysts for personal and professional development. By fostering this mindset, you not only combat negativity but also pave the way for a more fulfilling and resilient journey.

INTERACTIVE ELEMENT

ANTs Worksheet

1. Automatic Thought Record

- Identify the automatic negative thought (ANT).
- What triggered this thought?
- Rate the intensity of the thought on a scale from 1 to 10.
- Challenge the thought: Is there evidence supporting or contradicting this thought?

2. Decatastrophizing

- Describe the catastrophic thought.
- Ask yourself: What is the most adverse outcome possible?
- Explore the likelihood of this worst-case scenario.
- Generate alternative, more realistic outcomes.

3. Cataloging Your Inner Rules

- Identify a rule you have for yourself (e.g., "I must always please everyone").
- Examine the origin of this rule.
- Evaluate its impact on your well-being.
- Consider adopting a more flexible and realistic rule.

4. Facts or Opinions

- Write down a negative thought.
- Differentiate between facts and opinions in the thought.
- Challenge the opinions by questioning their validity.
- Rewrite the thought with a more balanced perspective.

5. The "Shoulds" Worksheet

- List "should" statements you often make (e.g., "I should be perfect").
- Explore the origin of these "should" statements.
- Evaluate the impact of these expectations on your mood.
- Replace unrealistic "shoulds" with more reasonable and compassionate statements.

Remember: Use this worksheet daily to confront and refute automatic negative thought patterns. Over time, regular practice will assist in cultivating a more resilient and optimistic outlook.

Test Your Thoughts

Meta-Modeling in NLP

Neuro-linguistic programming (NLP) introduces the concept of meta-modeling as a linguistic tool to uncover and challenge cognitive distortions. It involves questioning and clarifying language patterns to reveal the underlying structure of thoughts and beliefs. In the context of challenging automatic negative thoughts (ANTs), meta-modeling becomes a powerful technique to identify and address distorted thinking.

How Meta-Modeling Works

Meta-modeling operates by deconstructing vague or generalized language, which helps individuals explore the specifics of their thoughts. It aims to bring clarity to distorted thinking patterns, making room for more accurate perceptions and interpretations. By challenging the linguistic structure of thoughts, meta-modeling encourages a shift from limiting beliefs to more empowering and realistic perspectives.

Questions to Ask Yourself:

1. What assumptions am I making about this situation?
2. How did I arrive at this conclusion or belief?
3. Are there alternative explanations or interpretations?
4. What mental models or frameworks am I using to make sense of this?
5. How might someone with a different background or perspective see this situation?
6. Which biases could be shaping my thoughts?
7. Are there any logical fallacies in my reasoning?
8. What additional information or data could help refine my understanding?
9. How has my perspective evolved, and why?
10. Am I open to changing my views based on new information?

11. What are the potential consequences of my current beliefs or assumptions?
12. How do my emotions or feelings influence my interpretation?
13. Do I tend to generalize from specific instances?
14. Have I considered the context and nuances of the situation?
15. What feedback have I received from others regarding my interpretation?

These questions can help you engage in reflective thinking and refine your mental models, leading to a more nuanced and accurate understanding of the world around you.

After learning about the different ANTs and how to overcome them, it is now time, in the next chapter, to gain an understanding of emotional regulation. We will navigate the ebb and flow of emotions to gain control over the narrative that fuels anxious thoughts.

CHAPTER 4
A: ATTUNING TO YOUR EMOTIONS

The only thing we can do is play on the one string we have, and that is our attitude...I am convinced that life is 10% what happens to me and 90% how I react to it.

CHARLES R. SWINDOLL

The fact is, while we may not always have control over what happens to us, we possess the ability to choose our reactions. By focusing on maintaining a positive attitude, we can effectively navigate challenges and setbacks. Essentially, our responses to these situations play a much larger role in determining our overall well-being than the situations themselves. We should take ownership of our reactions and harness them to lead a fulfilling life.

EMOTIONAL REGULATION SKILLS

Emotional regulation involves controlling feelings through diverse strategies. Individuals with high emotional intelligence effectively manage both their own and others' emotions, employing coping mechanisms for self-regulation. This skill isn't innate but can be cultivated and refined over time, benefiting mental and physical health. Effective emotional regulation is crucial for adults navigating social expectations and daily challenges. Regulation challenges may stem from beliefs about negative emotions or a lack of skills, exacerbated by stressful situations, and emotional volatility can strain relationships, leading to regrettable actions and repairs. Uncontrolled emotions also harm individual well-being, causing suffering and hindering personal growth.

We can control our emotions by using a variety of strategies. Let's take a look at some!

- **Creating Space**

Emotions hit us like a speed train—no warning, just suddenly *bam*, we're angry or upset. So, the ultimate trick to handle these wild emotions is to hit the brakes. Give yourself a break, literally. Take a moment, catch your breath, and slow down that crazy rush between feeling triggered and reacting. It's like pressing pause on a hectic scene. This simple act of taking a beat can be a game-changer. It's like giving yourself a little gift—the power to choose how you react rather than being carried away by the emotional rollercoaster.

Pausing before reacting involves taking a momentary break before responding to a situation or stimulus. Instead of impulsively reacting, this practice allows us to create a space between the external trigger and our response. During this pause, you can reflect on emotions, consider the implications of different reactions, and choose a more thoughtful response. It develops self-control and prevents hasty, potentially regrettable actions. This deliberate pause provides an opportunity to approach situations with a calmer and more composed mindset, which leads to better decision-making and interpersonal interactions. Essentially, it's a strategic timeout to gain composure before engaging in a measured response.

- **Self-Awareness/Noticing How You Feel**

Developing emotional self-awareness involves recognizing and understanding your own feelings. Dr. Judson Brewer suggests developing curiosity about your physical reactions (Klynn, 2021). Pay attention to sensations in your body— whether it's an upset stomach, racing heart, or tension in your neck or head. These physical signals offer clues about your emotional condition. By exploring the connection between your physical and emotional experiences, you gain a better understanding of your feelings. This self-inquiry not only enhances emotional awareness but also serves as a distraction, helping to alleviate the intensity of emotions. To improve emotional self-awareness, regularly engage in practices that encourage the mindful observation of your bodily responses to emotions.

- **Naming How You Feel**

After recognizing your emotions, naming them is a powerful tool for gaining control. Ask yourself: What do I feel? Is it anger, sadness, disappointment, or resentment? Uncover underlying emotions, especially fear, that often lurk beneath others. Since we often experience multiple emotions simultaneously, identify them all. Then, delve deeper into each. If it's fear, pinpoint what you're afraid of. If it's anger, understand its source. Naming your emotions not only enhances self-awareness but also facilitates sharing them with others, which helps you take a crucial step toward effective communication and understanding.

- **Emotion Wheel**

The emotion wheel is an effective tool for improving emotional intelligence and enabling a better understanding of one's emotions. It typically consists of a circular diagram with a spectrum of emotions arranged in various categories. Users can pinpoint specific emotions they are experiencing by selecting from the wheel, helping them articulate their emotional states with greater precision. This tool is a visual aid that encourages individuals to explore the complexity of their feelings, going beyond basic labels like "happy" or "sad."

To utilize the emotion wheel effectively, begin by identifying a prominent emotion experienced in a given situation. As you move toward the outer edges of the wheel, you'll find nuanced variations of that primary emotion, which allow for a more detailed and accurate description of how you feel. This process promotes self-awareness and emotional literacy, which enables individuals to express themselves more precisely in both personal and interpersonal contexts. By regularly engaging with the emotion wheel, individuals can refine their emotional vocabulary and develop a heightened sensitivity to the range of emotions they encounter.

In practical terms, incorporating the emotion wheel into daily life involves pausing to reflect on feelings and consulting the wheel to identify and articulate them. This introspective practice fosters a deeper connection with one's emotional landscape and can be particularly beneficial in interpersonal communication, conflict resolution, and personal development.

- **Accepting the Emotion**

Emotions are like the colors of our inner world, painting our experiences with richness and depth. They are natural responses to the numerous situations that life presents us with. Instead of blaming ourselves for experiencing emotions, such as rage or anxiety, we must recognize that these feelings are totally real and understandable given the circumstances.

Engaging in self-compassion means treating yourself with kindness and understanding, especially when facing challenging circumstances. Instead of being harsh or judgmental toward yourself, offer grace by recognizing that it's okay to feel what you're feeling. To actively practice emotional acceptance, start by cultivating mindfulness. This means being present in the moment, acknowledging your emotions without judgment, and observing how they manifest physically in your body. By being mindful of your emotions, you open up room for acceptance.

Furthermore, it's important for you to release the belief that some emotions are inherently "good" or "bad." Embracing the concept that emotions constitute a natural aspect of human existence enables you to approach them with curiosity and openness. Engaging in self-reflection and probing your emotional experiences with questions can enhance your comprehension. By integrating these habits into your everyday routine, you empower yourself to navigate life's fluctuations with increased resilience and authenticity. This fosters a healthier and more compassionate connection with your own emotional terrain.

Questions to reflect on:

1. What emotions am I experiencing?
2. Where do I feel sensations in my body?
3. Am I judging my emotions?
4. How can I practice mindfulness right now?
5. What thoughts are emerging?
6. Can I offer myself compassion?
7. What can I accept right now?
8. What would it feel like to let go of control?
9. How can I nurture myself in this moment?
10. What can I learn from this emotional experience?

Try the exercise below if you want to successfully learn how to accept your feelings:

Time: Set aside at least 20 minutes for this exercise.

Materials: You can choose to follow along with your thoughts or use a journal. Keeping an emotion or mood journal aids in immersing yourself more profoundly in the experience.

1. Find a comfortable spot. Then, sit and take a few moments to slow your breath and calm your body. Practice long, deep breathing (inhale for four seconds, hold, then exhale for six seconds).
2. Recall a recent situation that evoked a strong emotion—sadness, grief, disappointment, anxiety, fear, anger, hurt, or frustration. Reflect on the trigger, the worst part, and your current sensations and emotions.
3. Pause, tune into the emotion, and write down your observations.
4. Observe the emotion and sensations with acceptance and curiosity. Notice changes and describe sensations, noting where sensations are strongest and their characteristics.
5. When judgmental thoughts arise, observe them as thoughts. Imagine them in front of you, detached. State, "I am having the thought that..." and recognize its impact on you.
6. Bring an attitude of tranquility and gentleness, accepting your experience without fixing or achieving a particular state. Offer words of self-compassion and empathy.

7. Reflect on what is difficult about allowing emotions to be present and what is helpful in this acceptance.

8. Soften your experience by holding distressing emotions with kindness, like a loving parent comforting a child. Name the emotion, say comforting words, and consider placing your hands on the area of your body with the strongest sensations.

9. Visualize a comforting form flowing into your body, surrounding the distressing emotions. Acknowledge that this part of you is worthy of comfort.

10. Focus on breathing for another minute. Breathe in (for a count of four) and breathe out (for a count of six). Let go of any lingering tension, allowing yourself to simply be.

Congratulations on completing this exercise! Take a moment to be proud of yourself for practicing accepting uncomfortable emotions. Journal about your experience, and consider actions to show yourself love, care, and support in the following days.

IDENTIFYING AND REDUCING EMOTIONAL TRIGGERS

Think of a trigger as something that sets off a strong emotional reaction in you, kind of like pushing a button that brings up intense feelings or memories. It could be anything from a certain smell or sound to a particular place or person. Triggers can suddenly make you feel overwhelmed with emotions or like you're reliving a past tough experience. Here are some examples of triggers:

- **Past Trauma:** If you've been through something really tough, anything that reminds you of that experience can be a trigger. It could be an accident, an abusive situation, or the loss of someone close to you.
- **Negative Memories:** Sometimes, memories of past failures, embarrassing moments, or disappointments can act as triggers, bringing back those same feelings of sadness, shame, or frustration.
- **Fear:** Phobias or fears you have can definitely be triggers. For instance, if you're terrified of heights, just the thought of being up high might make you feel anxious or panicky.
- **Stressful Situations:** Stress and anxiety can be triggered when you're under a lot of pressure or facing a tough situation. Things like tight deadlines at work or having to speak in public are common stress triggers.
- **Relationship Issues:** Interactions with certain people or reminders of past relationship problems can bring up strong emotions like sadness, anger, or resentment.
- **Loss or Grief:** Events or dates associated with losing someone or experiencing grief, like the anniversary of a loved one's passing, can trigger feelings of sadness or longing.
- **Change:** Big changes in your life, even if they're positive, can stir up a mix of emotions. Starting a new job, moving to a new place, or even getting into a new relationship can bring about excitement, anxiety, or stress.

So, triggers are like little emotional landmines that can catch you off guard and bring up all sorts of feelings from the past or present. It's important to recognize them and find healthy ways to cope when they pop up.

How Do Triggers Form?

In essence, researchers don't have a complete understanding of how or why the brain forms triggers, but they recognize that traumatic memories are encoded differently than non-traumatic ones. Traumatic events often linger just outside of our conscious memory, but our brain and body retain a record of these threatening experiences.

To safeguard against potential harm in the future, our brains link the fight-or-flight response to reminders of trauma, such as specific smells, sights, or sounds. When exposed to these triggers, we react as if we are in immediate danger, leading to a response akin to symptoms seen in post-traumatic stress disorder (PTSD).

The process of trigger formation generally unfolds as follows:

1. **Experience:** An event or situation occurs that triggers a powerful emotional reaction, spanning from a distressing incident to a joyful occasion.
2. **Association:** Over time, certain stimuli (like sounds, smells, places, or people) become subconsciously linked with emotional responses.
3. **Memory:** The brain stores these associations in memory. This explains why specific triggers can

provoke intense emotional responses, even if the original event happened a long time ago.

4. **Triggering:** Later, when exposed to the same or similar stimuli, these triggers can evoke the same emotional response linked to the original event. This can happen even if the person is not consciously aware of the connection between the stimulus and the initial experience.

All in all, triggers are formed through a complex process of association and memory encoding, wherein certain stimuli become linked to emotionally charged experiences. The brain then reacts strongly to these triggers, often inducing a fight-or-flight response, even when the threat is not present. This mechanism plays a role in conditions like PTSD, where the emotional impact of a traumatic event continues to affect an individual long after the event itself.

How to Recognize Emotional Triggers

Recognizing triggers involves being attuned to unexpected emotional responses or shifts in your well-being and understanding that these reactions might be linked to specific events or circumstances. Triggers can manifest in various forms, ranging from seemingly minor disruptions to more significant life events. Here are some ways to identify your triggers:

- **Notice How You Feel**

Pay attention to your emotions. If you suddenly feel anxious, overwhelmed, or find it challenging to calm yourself down without a clear reason, it could be a sign that you're triggered. These emotions may feel sudden and unrelated to your current situation.

- **Listen to Yourself**

If you find yourself repeatedly venting about a specific issue, even after you believe you've mentally moved on, it could be a sign of a trigger. Incessant rehashing suggests that something about the situation may still be affecting you on a deeper level.

- **Check Your Feelings**

Be mindful of the intensity of your reactions. If your responses seem disproportionately strong or explosive, it might indicate that you're not reacting solely to the immediate circumstances but also to an underlying stressor.

- **Something Is Bothering You**

Take note of any issue that suddenly weighs on your mind. While major concerns may be expected, if a routine occurrence is causing stress, it might indicate an underlying trigger. Acknowledge whether or not there's more to your stress than meets the eye.

How to Deal With Emotional Triggers

Dealing with emotional triggers involves more than just addressing immediate reactions. While short-term strategies can help in the moment, it's essential to employ long-term solutions for lasting coping mechanisms. Here are some enduring strategies to handle emotional triggers:

- **Practice Mindfulness**

Nurture mindfulness by being fully present in the current moment. Pay close attention to your emotions and stay mentally prepared through practices like meditation or yoga. This allows you to become more attuned to your triggers, and this heightened awareness equips you with stronger coping mechanisms.

- **Recognize Toxic Relationships**

Identify and acknowledge relationships that consistently bring negativity into your life. In a toxic relationship, mutual understanding, respect, and consideration are lacking. Recognizing these relationships and addressing these problems are crucial for long-term emotional well-being.

- **Maintain a Mood Journal**

While writing may seem cumbersome, keeping a mood journal can be a therapeutic and insightful practice. Documenting your feelings helps recognize patterns related to emotional triggers. This written record becomes a valuable guide for positive changes and avoiding future triggers.

- **Seek Professional Help**

Developing emotional self-regulation can be tough. While early education on self-regulation helps, some triggers may be deeply rooted, making it hard for you to recognize them. Seeking professional therapy offers a safe and non-judgmental environment to explore and understand these triggers. Therapists provide you with support, guidance, and effective strategies to manage emotions and promote healing. Therapy becomes a valuable resource for you during your journey of emotional self-discovery and recovery.

THE ABCS OF EMOTIONAL REGULATION

You can utilize the ABCs as tools to help you effectively manage your emotions. They are designed to decrease vulnerability to intense emotions and boost your emotional resilience. The acronym ABC represents the three key components of these skills:

A: Accumulate Positive Emotions

This involves intentionally and regularly incorporating positive and enjoyable activities into your life. The goal is to create a balance between immediate contentment and enduring fulfillment. It's about ensuring that you have a mix of activities that bring joy and fulfillment into your life.

Regularly participate in activities that bring you joy and are consistent with your ideals. These activities should enhance both short-term satisfaction and long-term fulfillment. This could include activities like hobbies, spending time with loved ones, or following personal interests.

B: Build Mastery

Mastery refers to the sense of accomplishment and success one feels when achieving a goal. While children often naturally seek out mastery experiences, as teens and adults, it requires intentional effort. Building mastery involves actively pursuing and succeeding in tasks or activities that challenge you, contributing to a sense of competence and achievement.

Actively seek out tasks or activities that challenge you and allow for a sense of accomplishment. This could involve learning new skills, setting and achieving goals, or taking on challenges that push your boundaries.

C: Cope Ahead

Anticipating emotionally challenging situations and coping ahead involves planning and preparing for how you will navigate these situations. It's a conscious and intentional process that often includes visualizing yourself in the upcoming scenario and strategically planning the coping strategies you will employ to manage and overcome potential emotional challenges.

Prepare for emotionally hard situations. Visualization can be an effective tool in this process. Consider the probable issues you may encounter and devise a strategy for efficiently dealing with them. Plan out unique coping techniques that are compatible with your emotional well-being.

The way the ABCs work is by getting people to consider how their thoughts and feelings are related. People can learn more about why they feel the way they do by pinpointing the activation event and the ideas that surround it. This knowledge makes it possible to question and reinterpret unreasonable or harmful beliefs, which eventually results in a more stable and productive emotional reaction.

Helpful Tips:

- **Put Mindfulness Into Practice**

Develop a judgment-free awareness of your ideas and feelings so that you can more objectively observe your thoughts and behaviors by practicing mindfulness.

- **Make Use of Journals**

To keep track of beliefs, activating events, and outcomes, keep a journal. Clarity and insight into reoccurring patterns can be obtained by putting things in writing.

- **Seek Assistance**

Never be afraid to ask a therapist or a reliable friend for help and direction when using the ABC skill. They can help you see things from a different angle and dispel false ideas.

- **Have Patience**

Changing deeply rooted mental habits requires work and patience. As you practice the ABC skill, be kind to yourself and acknowledge your little accomplishments along the way.

- **Exercise Self-Compassion**

Be gentle and sympathetic to yourself, especially when confronting ideas that lead to bad feelings. Remind yourself that everything will be alright.

WORRY POSTPONEMENT

Worry postponement is a cognitive strategy aimed at managing anxiety and enhancing emotional regulation. Instead of allowing worrisome thoughts to overwhelm you in the present moment, consciously choose to delay them to a designated time in the future. This technique encourages a sense of control over your thoughts and emotions, preventing them from dominating your immediate experiences and disrupting your emotional well-being.

How It Helps With Emotional Regulation

Worry postponement offers several benefits for emotional regulation. By postponing worry, you grant yourself the mental space needed to engage with your current circumstances more effectively. This practice allows you to distance yourself from overwhelming emotions, preventing them from hijacking your present experiences. As a result, you gain better control over your emotional responses, which leads to a more balanced and composed state of mind. Furthermore, setting aside dedicated time for worry can provide clarity and context, enabling you to address concerns more rationally and constructively.

How to Postpone Your Worry

To postpone worry, start by acknowledging your anxious thoughts as they arise. Then, instead of immediately delving into them, tell yourself that you will address these concerns later. Choose a specific time and place for worry, perhaps allocating 15 minutes at the end of the day. During this designated period, allow yourself to explore and process your worries without judgment. This deliberate approach prevents the intrusion of worrisome thoughts throughout the day, allowing you to focus on the present moment.

Helpful Tips / Dos and Don'ts

Dos:

1. **Set a Specific Time:** Choose a consistent time for worry postponement, creating a structured approach.
2. **Create a Worry List:** Jot down concerns as they arise, saving them for the designated worry time.
3. **Mindfulness Techniques:** Incorporate mindfulness practices to stay present and avoid getting swept away by worry.
4. **Problem-Solving during Worry Time:** Use the designated time to explore solutions and take actionable steps to address worries.

Don'ts:

1. **Postpone Indefinitely:** Don't procrastinate addressing worries indefinitely. Set a reasonable time frame to maintain effectiveness.
2. **Engage in Catastrophic Thinking:** Resist the urge to catastrophize during the worry period. Focus on realistic assessments and solutions.
3. **Constantly Reschedule Worry Time:** Stick to the allocated time to prevent the worry period from bleeding into the entire day.

4. **Judge Yourself for Worrying:** Embrace a non-judgmental attitude toward your worries. Remember, everyone experiences concerns, and postponement is a tool for managing them, not eradicating them.

In adopting worry postponement, you empower yourself to navigate daily challenges with greater emotional resilience, enhancing overall well-being and mental clarity.

INTERACTIVE ELEMENT

Emotional Regulation Worksheet

With the help of this worksheet, you can discover your feelings, investigate coping strategies, and create a customized plan for emotional control.

1. Recognizing Your Emotions

- Take a moment to reflect on your current emotional state.
- Identify the primary emotions you are experiencing (e.g., anger, sadness, anxiety).
- Assign a numerical value on a scale from 1 to 10 to indicate the intensity of each emotion.

Emotion: _____ Intensity: _____

Emotion: _____ Intensity: _____

Emotion: _____ Intensity: _____

2. Understanding Triggers

- Think about what situations or events triggered these emotions.
- Find any patterns or repeated themes in your emotional triggers.
- Consider how your thoughts and interpretations contribute to these emotional responses.

Trigger: _____

Trigger: _____

Trigger: _____

3. Coping Strategies

- Brainstorm a list of coping strategies that have helped you regulate your emotions in the past.
- Include both short-term strategies for immediate relief and long-term strategies for ongoing emotional well-being.
- Consider methods like deep breathing, mindfulness, engaging in physical exercise, expressing creativity, and reaching out for social support.

Coping Strategy: _____

Coping Strategy: _____

Coping Strategy: _____

4. Developing a Regulation Plan

- Based on your identified emotions, triggers, and coping strategies, create a personalized emotional regulation plan.
- Outline specific steps you can take to regulate your emotions when faced with triggering situations.
- Include both proactive strategies to prevent emotional escalation and reactive strategies to manage intense emotions in the moment.

Regulation Plan

- Before a Trigger

  - Practice mindfulness meditation for five minutes each morning.
  - Identify potential triggers and develop coping strategies.

- During a Trigger

  - To improve focus, take three deep breaths.
  - Remember that feelings are fleeting and will pass.
  - Reframe negative thoughts with encouraging words for yourself.

- After a Trigger

  - Reflect on the situation and your emotional response.
  - Practice self-compassion and forgiveness.

○ Engage in a relaxing activity to restore emotional balance.

5. Commitment to Practice

- Commit to consistently implementing your emotional regulation plan.
- Set realistic goals for incorporating coping strategies into your daily routine.
- Monitor your progress and adjust your plan as needed based on what works best for you.

Commitment Statement

I commit to prioritizing my emotional well-being by practicing the coping strategies outlined in this plan. I will remain mindful of my emotions, utilize effective regulation techniques, and seek support when needed to cultivate greater emotional resilience and overall happiness.

Anchoring Waves of Emotion

Anchoring in neuro-linguistic programming (NLP) is a technique that associates a specific stimulus with a particular emotional state or resourceful state. Essentially, it involves creating a link between an external trigger (anchor) and an internal emotional response. When applied effectively, anchoring can be a powerful tool for emotional regulation, helping individuals intentionally access desired emotional states. Types of anchoring include:

1. **Visual Anchors:** This involves associating an emotion with a specific visual cue. For example, looking at a picture that invokes feelings of calmness.
2. **Auditory Anchors:** This involves linking an emotion to a particular sound or tone. This could be a specific piece of music or a calming phrase.
3. **Kinesthetic Anchors:** This involves tying an emotion to a physical sensation, like a specific touch, gesture, or body movement.

How to Use Anchoring for Emotional Regulation

1. Choose Your Desired Feeling

- Decide on the emotion you want to cultivate, such as calmness or relaxation, to reduce anxiety.

2. Recall a Peaceful Moment

- Reflect on an experience where you felt deeply calm and connected to the present moment.

3. Select a Sensory Anchor

- Choose a sensory anchor, like smell. An example of this is using an essential oil inhaler.

4. Immerse Yourself in the Memory

- Recall the details of the calming memory, by visualizing what you saw, heard, and felt in that moment.

5. Relive the Experience

- Dive deep into the memory until you begin to feel the same sense of calmness and relaxation.

6. Apply Mental Anchoring

- When you reach peak relaxation, use the sensory anchor. Inhale slowly and deeply from the essential oil inhaler to reinforce the positive feeling.

7. Test the Anchor

- Assess the effectiveness of the anchor by using the inhaler without recalling the calm memory. Notice if you can still induce a relaxing state.

8. Practice and Repetition

- Understand that achieving results may require multiple attempts. Consistent repetition is key to strengthening the mental anchor and its association with the desired feeling.

Now that we understand the importance of emotional regulation and how tow to effectively regulate our emotions, in the next chapter, we'll delve into the various stress and time management strategies. This will help us protect ourselves from stressors so that we're in the best headspace to make sound decisions.

OVERTHINKING & ANXIETY? THINK AGAIN
REVIEW PAGE

"In the vast garden of humanity, where kindness blooms unceasingly, lies a profound truth: those who give without expectation often discover their lives enriched beyond measure."

Picture a journey where every small act of kindness becomes a stepping stone towards deeper connections and greater contentment.

So, I ask you: Would you extend a hand to a stranger, even if your gesture went unnoticed?

Who might this stranger be? Perhaps not so different from you – someone seeking guidance, grappling with uncertainty, yearning for a helping hand.

My mission is crystal clear: to demystify the complexities of Overthinking & Anxiety for everyone. Every effort I make is in service of this goal. And to achieve it, we need to reach... well... everyone.

That's where you come in. Let's be real – most people do judge a book by its cover (and its reviews). So, here's my humble ask on behalf of a fellow traveler in the Overthinking & Anxiety community...

Could you spare a moment to share your thoughts through a review of this book?

★ ★ ★ ★ ★

Your act costs nothing but a minute of your time. Yet, its impact could be profound. Your words might lead to:

...another person finding clarity in their mental struggles. ...another soul finding solace within these pages amidst life's chaos. ...another step forward on the journey of self-discovery and resilience. ...another triumph over doubts and fears.

To lend a hand and truly make a difference, all it takes is less than 60 seconds to leave a review.

Simply scan the QR code below to share your thoughts:

If the idea of helping a fellow member of the Overthinking & Anxiety community resonates with you, then welcome aboard. You're one of us.

I'm excited to guide you toward conquering Overthinking & Anxiety. Get ready for the wisdom, strategies, and insights waiting for you in the pages ahead.

With sincere gratitude,

Your ally in the pursuit of inner peace, Dean.

Dean Middlbergh

PS - Just a heads up: Sharing knowledge not only helps others but also enriches your own journey. If you believe this book could benefit someone else, consider passing it along. Sharing is a gift that gives back to both the giver and receiver.

Now, let's get back to our regularly scheduled programming.

CHAPTER 5

I: INHALE, EXHALE, REPEAT

Within you, there is a stillness and a sanctuary to which you can retreat at any time and be yourself.

HERMANN HESSE

STRESS AND OVERTHINKING

Stress stems from various aspects of life, and it affects everyone differently. Within this web of stress triggers, you may find yourself grappling with financial pressures and navigating the demanding landscapes of the modern workplace. The relentless competition, strict deadlines, and the constant pursuit of excellence create a breeding ground for stress, where the fear of job insecurity adds to the pressure on your delicate balance between professional aspirations and personal well-being.

Financial pressures cast a long shadow, which generates pervasive stress as you strive to meet obligations and fear economic downturns, causing a constant undercurrent of anxiety. This financial stress seeps into different facets of life, impacting relationships and mental health.

Interpersonal dynamics, both in personal and professional spheres, contribute significantly to stress in your life. Conflicts, misunderstandings, and the effort to maintain meaningful connections in an increasingly virtual world add emotional burdens. Balancing personal relationships with other life responsibilities adds complexity, which leads to stress in the delicate interplay of human connections.

The fragility of human health becomes a potent stress catalyst, as chronic illnesses, sudden medical emergencies, or the daily upkeep of physical well-being induce stress. The fear of the unknown, coupled with vulnerability to health-related uncertainties, becomes a persistent source of emotional turmoil.

Societal expectations exert a strong influence on your stress levels. The pressure to conform to societal standards in appearance, achievements, or life milestones can be overwhelming, and constantly comparing yourself to societal ideals and the fear of falling short contribute to a pervasive sense of inadequacy and stress.

Recognizing and understanding these stress triggers is crucial for developing effective coping mechanisms. Yet, stress seldom exists in isolation; it often intertwines with another formidable challenge—overthinking. The relentless cognitive processes associated with overthinking amplify stressors, intensifying their impact. As you grapple with stress, your mind may engage in incessant rumination, creating hypothetical scenarios and magnifying the perceived severity of the stressors.

Relationship Between Stress and Overthinking

When you're stressed, it's like your mind hits overdrive. You start thinking about the problem from every angle, replaying scenarios endlessly in your head. Picture it like this: You encounter a stressful situation, which triggers a cascade of thoughts. As stress takes hold, your mind seeks to understand and resolve the problem; however, in doing so, plunges into overthinking. This overanalysis, in turn, exacerbates the stress you initially faced. The more you ruminate, the more stress intensifies, creating a self-perpetuating loop.

Stress serves as the instigator, planting the seeds of doubt and concern in your mind. It might be triggered by work pressures, financial strains, or interpersonal conflicts. As stress creeps in, your mind, in its attempt to grapple with the situation, starts overthinking. You find yourself entangled in a web of hypothetical scenarios and incessant analysis, each thought intensifying the emotional impact of the stressor. The more you overthink, the more stress gains a foothold, turning a manageable challenge into an overwhelming ordeal.

This overthinking only adds fuel to the fire of stress. Instead of finding solutions, you end up dwelling on the issue, making it seem bigger and more overwhelming than it actually is. Your thoughts become consumed by what-ifs and worst-case scenarios, feeding your anxiety even more. It's as if your mind becomes fixated on the problem, unable to let it go. You keep turning it over and over in your head, unable to find a way out of the mental loop. This constant rumination not only heightens your stress levels but also drains your mental energy, leaving you feeling exhausted and overwhelmed. When caught in a cycle of rumination, you dwell on the stressor, magnifying its significance and elongating its mental presence. This heightened focus on the stressor, fueled by overthinking, amplifies its emotional toll. Consequently, the stress that initially triggered the overthinking is now compounded, deepening its roots and becoming more entrenched in your psyche.

Furthermore, excessive overthinking frequently originates from a fear of uncertainties. When you experience stress, there's a tendency to fret about potential future events and outcomes. You play out different scenarios in your mind, trying to anticipate every possible outcome. But instead of providing clarity, this endless speculation only increases your anxiety, and you become trapped in a cycle of worry, unable to break free from the grip of your own thoughts.

Another way overthinking fuels stress is by preventing you from switching off. Even when you try to relax, your mind continues to race, replaying conversations, analyzing situations, and second-guessing decisions. It's like there's a constant chatter in your head, making it impossible to find peace and quiet. This persistent mental activity not only prevents you from unwinding but also contributes to feelings of restlessness and agitation.

Ultimately, you find yourself caught in a vicious cycle between stress and overthinking. Stress triggers overthinking, and in response, overthinking intensifies stress, forming a challenging feedback loop that may be hard for you to break free from.

Signs of Stress

When stress starts to seep into your life, it often leaves behind a trail of subtle but significant signs. These signs serve as red flags, indicating that your mental and emotional well-being may be under strain.

- **Depressed Mood**

When stress takes hold, you may notice a persistent shift in your emotional landscape. A prevailing sense of sadness or despondency might settle in, casting a shadow over daily experiences. Recognizing and acknowledging this shift is crucial, as it serves as an initial signal that stress might be exerting its influence.

- **Chronic Anxiety**

Stress and anxiety often go hand in hand, creating a perpetual cycle of worry and apprehension. If you find yourself caught in a web of anxious thoughts, constantly anticipating the next challenge or problem, it may be a clear indication that stress has infiltrated your mental state.

- **Difficulty Sleeping (or Sleeping Too Much)**

Your sleep patterns can serve as a reliable barometer of stress. You may experience insomnia, finding it challenging to fall or stay asleep, especially during stressful periods.

Conversely, an uptick in the need for extra sleep could also signal your body's response to elevated stress levels.

- **Irritability**

Stress has a way of fraying nerves, making irritability a common companion. You might find yourself becoming easily agitated, reacting more intensely to minor inconveniences, or experiencing heightened sensitivity to external stimuli. These moments of irritability can be indicative of an underlying stress burden.

- **Difficulty Concentrating, Focusing, or Learning**

The cognitive effects of stress can manifest in various ways, impacting your ability to concentrate and focus. If you notice a decline in your attention span, ability to process information, or ability to learn new material, stress may be exerting its influence on your mental faculties.

- **Insomnia**

The inability to achieve restful sleep can be a direct consequence of stress. If your mind races with worries, preventing the tranquility needed for a good night's sleep, insomnia may become a prevalent feature of your daily life.

- **Stress Eating, Bingeing, or Increasing Substance Intake**

Stress can manifest in unhealthy coping mechanisms, such as changes in eating habits or increased reliance on substances like drugs or alcohol. If you find yourself resorting to these behaviors as a means of alleviating stress, it's crucial to recognize these patterns and seek healthier alternatives.

- **Loss of Sex Drive**

Stress has the power to infiltrate various aspects of your life, including your intimate relationships. A noticeable decline in your sex drive might be an indication that stress is impacting not only your emotional well-being but also your physical connection with others.

STRESSING THE VALUE OF STRESS MANAGEMENT FOR MENTAL CLARITY

Grounding Techniques

When stress takes hold, grounding techniques offer a powerful way to reconnect with the present moment and regain a sense of control. Here's your personalized, step-by-step guide for physical, mental, and soothing grounding techniques:

Physical Grounding

1. **Feel Your Feet:** Find a comfortable seated or standing position. Close your eyes and shift your focus to your feet. Notice the sensation as they connect with the ground. Wiggle your toes and sense the stability beneath you. This simple act anchors you to the physical world.

2. **Touch and Texture:** Engage your sense of touch. Hold onto an object nearby—it could be a smooth stone, a textured fabric, or even the surface of a table. Feel its contours, temperature, and weight. Let this tactile experience divert your attention from stress.

3. **Body Scan:** Bring awareness to different parts of your body, starting with your toes, and then moving up through your legs, torso, arms, and head. As you exhale, pay attention to any tension or discomfort in your body. Consciously release the tension as you exhale, allowing yourself to relax.

Mental Grounding

1. **Five Senses Check-In:** Take a moment to engage each of your five senses. What are you currently seeing, hearing, smelling, tasting, and touching? This sensory exploration pulls your focus away from stressful thoughts, anchoring you in the richness of your immediate environment.

2. **Name Game:** Engage your mind by identifying elements in your surroundings. Notice five things you can see, touch four items, listen for three sounds, detect two scents, and identify one taste. This mental exercise redirects your focus, providing a reprieve from stressors.

3. **Counting and Math:** Perform a simple counting exercise. Choose a number and count backward or forward, focusing solely on the numbers. Alternatively, engage in basic mental math, diverting your thoughts from stress while stimulating your cognitive functions.

Soothing Grounding

1. **Visualization:** Close your eyes and envision a peaceful place, like a beach, a forest, or any serene setting. Imagine the sights, sounds, and smells in vivid detail. As you immerse yourself in this mental sanctuary, let go of stress and embrace tranquility.

2. **Affirmations:** Create positive affirmations like "I am calm and in control" or "I can handle whatever comes my way" to counteract stress. By affirming positivity, you redirect your mind toward constructive thoughts, fostering a more resilient mindset.

3. **Self-Compassion Break:** Place your hand over your heart, acknowledging any emotional pain or stress. Speak kindly to yourself, recognizing that challenges are a part of life. Provide comforting words to yourself, just as you would to a friend experiencing distress. Embracing this self-compassionate approach fosters emotional well-being.

Mindfulness Practices

Mindfulness is a state of purposeful, nonjudgmental attention to the present moment. Mindfulness skills are frequently applied to other activities, such as yoga and meditation. Here are some popular mindfulness exercises—many of these can be tried anywhere, at home or on the go.

Breathwork

- **Deep Breathing**

Engaging in deep breathing is a simple yet powerful technique to cultivate a sense of calm. Make yourself comfortable by either lying down or sitting, ensuring that you are relaxed. Inhale slowly through your nose, guiding the breath deep into your belly. As you breathe in, feel your abdomen rise, expanding with the inflow of air. Then, exhale through your nose, allowing your belly to gently fall. To improve your awareness, place one hand on your belly and the other on your chest; make sure that the hand on your belly moves more than the one on your chest. Repeat this mindful breathing process for three more cycles, concentrating on the rhythmic rise and fall of your abdomen.

- **Breath Focus**

Embark on a journey to tranquility by incorporating breath focus into your relaxation routine. Begin by closing your eyes, shutting out external stimuli. Take deliberate, deep breaths, fostering a connection between your breath and inner calmness. Visualize a serene landscape or scenario that exudes peace. Inhale, immersing yourself in the imagined tranquility, then exhale, releasing stress with each breath. Integrate a chosen phrase with your breath, silently repeating "I breathe in peace and calmness" during inhalation and "I breathe out stress and tension" upon exhalation. Sustain this meditative practice for a duration of 10 to 20 minutes, allowing the harmonious rhythm of your breath guide you into a state of serenity.

- **Equal-Time Breathing**

Equal-time breathing helps you breathe in harmony and cultivates mindfulness and balance. While sitting comfortably, make sure your spine is straight. Take a deep breath through your nose and count to five. In the same count of five, simultaneously release the breath through your nose. Repeat multiple times in a rhythmic breathing pattern. As you get more comfortable with this exercise, progressively increase the length of each breath, going from 5 counts to 10 counts or more. By gradually extending, you can learn to regulate your breathing, which promotes attention and relaxation.

- **Modified Lion's Breath**

The modified lion's breath is a dynamic technique that helps you channel your inner strength and create a sense of liberation. Sit comfortably and center yourself in the present moment as you prepare to start. Breathe in deeply through your nose, letting the air fill your belly. Open your mouth wide and let out a strong "HA" sound at the top of your inhale to let out any stored stress. Embrace the image of yourself as a lion as you take numerous deep breaths like this one, exhaling firmly and letting go of tension with each "HA." This practice gives you a renewed sensation of energy and empowerment in addition to improving your breathing.

Progressive Muscle Relaxation

Progressive Muscle Relaxation (PMR) proves to be a convenient technique that can be easily executed in the comfort of your home, requiring no special equipment. All that's necessary is focused attention and a serene environment free from distractions.

Script 1

1. Find a comfortable spot to sit or lie down. You can center yourself by inhaling deeply through your nose and exhaling through your mouth.
2. Focus on your feet. Curl your toes, hold briefly, then release. Feel warmth and relaxation flow through your feet.
3. Move to your calves. Point your toes toward your head, tense briefly, then release to allow full relaxation.
4. Shift to your thighs. Tighten briefly, then let go to allow your thighs to loosen and relax.
5. Move up to your buttocks. Squeeze, hold, then release, feeling tension melt away.
6. Bring attention to your abdomen. Tighten, hold, and then release, allowing complete relaxation.
7. Shift to your chest and upper back. Inhale deeply, hold, then exhale, releasing tension in your chest and upper back.
8. Focus on your hands. Clench your fists, hold, and release, letting tension leave your hands.
9. Move to your arms and biceps. Tighten briefly then release, letting your arms become limp.
10. Shift to your shoulders. Shrug up, hold, and release, feeling relaxation spread across your shoulders.
11. Focus on your neck. Tilt your head back, hold, then bring it back to the center, releasing tension.

12. Finally, focus on your face. Scrunch your facial muscles, hold, then release, allowing your face to soften.
13. Enjoy the overall relaxation. When ready, open your eyes and return to the present moment.

Script 2

1. Locate a peaceful area, then close your eyes and engage in deep breaths. Concentrate on the inhalation and exhalation as you allow yourself to be present in the moment.
2. Begin with your feet. Inhale, tense your feet muscles, and as you exhale, release. Observe the difference between the feelings of tension and relaxation that you experience.
3. Move to your calves. Inhale, tense, and exhale. While you exhale, let go of any tension. Be present with the relaxation in your calves.
4. Shift to your thighs. Inhale deeply, tense, and exhale, releasing tension. Feel warmth and relaxation in your thighs.
5. Focus on your abdomen by inhaling, tightening, and exhaling, dissolving tension. Notice the gentle rise and fall of your breath.
6. Move to your chest and upper back. Inhale deeply, fill your lungs, then exhale to release tightness. Feel your breath nourishing your body.
7. Shift to your hands. Inhale, clench your fists, and exhale, releasing tension. Feel openness and ease in your hands.

8. Move to your arms and biceps. Inhale, tense, and exhale, allowing any tension to melt away. Notice relaxation in your arms.

9. Shift to your shoulders. Inhale, shrug up, and then exhale, letting them drop. Feel the weight lifting off your shoulders.

10. Focus on your neck. Inhale, tilt your head back, and exhale, bringing your head back to the center to release neck tension.

11. Finally, focus on your face. Inhale, scrunch your facial muscles, and exhale, releasing tension. Feel the softness and calmness in your face.

12. Be present in the relaxed sensation felt throughout your entire body. Open your eyes and bring yourself back to a clear, concentrated state of mind when you feel ready.

Body Scan

Engaging in a body scan meditation is a straightforward and accessible form of mindfulness. Here's a simplified guide to help you begin:

1. Set the Scene

Find a comfortable position, ideally lying down, especially if you're incorporating a body scan meditation into your bedtime routine. However, sitting comfortably is also an acceptable alternative.

2. Preparation With Breath

Take a moment to settle in and take a few deep breaths. Allow your breathing to slow down, emphasizing belly breathing rather than chest breathing. Envision yourself experiencing the rhythmic expansion and contraction of your abdomen with every breath, resembling the inflation and deflation of a balloon. Shift your focus away from your shoulders rising and falling.

3. Focus on Your Feet

Direct your awareness to your feet. Begin to observe any sensations in this area. If you encounter discomfort or pain, acknowledge it along with any associated thoughts or emotions. Breathe gently through these sensations, allowing yourself to remain present.

4. Breathe Into Tension

If you observe any uncomfortable sensations, intentionally focus your attention on them. Inhale into these areas, visualizing tension dissipating and evaporating into the air with each breath. Progress to the next area when you feel prepared.

5. Scan Your Entire Body

Extend this practice to each part of your body, gradually ascending from your feet to the crown of your head. Be attentive to how you feel and identify areas where stress may be held. In the presence of tightness, pain, or pressure, continue to breathe into these sensations. This not only aids in immediate tension release but also cultivates awareness for future tension management.

The essence of a body scan lies in the gentle exploration of sensations throughout your body. By mindfully addressing discomfort and utilizing breath as a tool for release, you foster a deeper connection with your bodily experiences. This practice not only facilitates relaxation in the moment but also enhances your awareness of tension, enabling you to manage it more effectively in the future.

Meditation

Meditating can help you develop inner peace, lower stress levels, and improve your general well-being. It is a life-changing practice. Choose a quiet area to sit comfortably so that you can maintain a straight spine, and place your hands lightly on your lap or knees before starting your meditation practice. You should then close your eyes and focus on your breathing. Breathe in deeply, letting the fresh air fill your lungs, and then gently breathe out, letting go of any stress. Let's now look at a few meditation scripts that will help you along the way.

- **Mindful Breathing**

As you pay attention to your breath, observe the refreshing sensation while you breathe in and the comforting warmth as you breathe out. Let each breath anchor you in the present moment. If your mind begins to stray, gently guide it back to the sensation of your breathing. With each breath, feel a sense of calmness washing over you. You are fully present, alive, embracing the tranquility of this moment.

- **Body Scan Meditation**

Begin by focusing your awareness on your toes, picturing a warm, relaxing light surrounding them. Gradually shift your attention upward, releasing tension in your feet, ankles, and calves. Progress through each part of your body—your knees, thighs, abdomen, chest, arms, neck, and head. Experience the calming energy flowing through each area, inducing profound relaxation. By doing this, you are grounding yourself in the present moment, establishing a full connection with your body.

- **Loving-Kindness Meditation**

Start by centering your thoughts on someone dear to you. Visualize their face, feel their presence, and extend heartfelt well-wishes: "May you be happy, healthy, safe, and at ease." Gradually broaden these wishes to include yourself, friends, family, acquaintances, and even those you find challenging. Acknowledge that all beings are interconnected as you exude kindness and love. You become a conduit of positive energy, nurturing compassion and understanding.

Guided Imagery/Visualization

Script 1: The Tranquil Meadow

In a quiet space, make yourself comfortable by sitting or lying down. Close your eyes, breathe deeply, and picture yourself in a serene meadow, surrounded by vibrant flowers.

Feel the grass beneath your feet, hear the rustling leaves, and picture a calm pond reflecting the serene sky. Sit by the water, releasing tension with each breath. Inhale the meadow's tranquility, exhale stress. Allow the peaceful energy to envelop you, cultivating a profound sense of inner peace.

Script 2: The Ocean Retreat

Sit in a comfortable position and close your eyes. Envision yourself on a quiet, secluded beach with golden sand. The rhythmic sound of gentle waves fills the air, creating a calming symphony. Feel the warm sand beneath your fingers as you sit and watch the waves gracefully rolling in. Picture the sun setting on the horizon, casting a spectrum of colors across the sky. Imagine yourself walking toward the water's edge, allowing the waves to wash over your feet, carrying away any stress or worries. As you watch the sunset, feel a deep sense of relaxation and peace settling within you; visualize the ocean absorbing any tension, leaving you with a profound sense of calmness.

PRIORITIZATION AND DECISION-MAKING

The ability to prioritize effectively and make informed decisions is crucial for personal and professional success. The demands on our time seem to be ever-increasing, and the constant flow of information can be overwhelming. This is where the art of prioritization, coupled with efficient time management, comes into play.

How Time Management Reduces Stress and Improves Decision-Making

- **Reducing Overwhelm:** Effective time management offers a key benefit: reducing overwhelm. When you're facing a mountain of tasks, it's natural to feel stressed and stuck. Prioritizing tasks by urgency and importance helps you break down the workload into manageable chunks, easing the burden.
- **Enhancing Focus:** Time management encourages focused work on one task at a time. This approach prevents the scattering of attention across multiple activities, allowing for a deeper level of concentration. As a result, decision-making becomes more precise, informed, and less prone to errors.
- **Creating a Sense of Control:** Knowing how to allocate your time effectively creates a sense of control in your daily life. This control is a powerful antidote to stress, as it instills confidence in your ability to handle tasks and make decisions in a timely manner.
- **Preventing Procrastination:** Procrastination is a common source of stress. By implementing time management techniques, you can tackle tasks systematically, eliminating the temptation to put things off. This proactive approach to responsibilities minimizes stress and increases the likelihood of making well-thought-out decisions.

Time Management or Prioritization Techniques

1. The Eisenhower Matrix

Named after former U.S. President Dwight D. Eisenhower, this matrix stands as a formidable instrument for classifying tasks according to their urgency and importance. It categorizes tasks into four quadrants: those that are both urgent and important, important but not urgent, urgent but not important, and those that are neither urgent nor important. By prioritizing tasks according to these criteria, individuals can focus on what truly matters and avoid the trap of constantly firefighting urgent but unimportant tasks.

Implementing the Eisenhower Matrix begins with a thorough assessment of one's to-do list. By categorizing tasks into the matrix, individuals gain clarity on where to direct their immediate attention versus what can be scheduled for later. This approach helps prevent the stress of feeling overwhelmed by tasks that may seem urgent but lack genuine importance.

2. Pomodoro Technique

You can employ the Pomodoro Technique, developed by Francesco Cirillo, as a time management strategy. This approach encourages you to break down tasks into intervals, usually lasting 25 minutes, with short breaks in between. These time segments are referred to as "Pomodoros." Following the completion of four Pomodoros, a more extended break of 15–30 minutes is scheduled.

The technique leverages the human brain's ability to maintain focus for short durations, preventing burnout and enhancing productivity. By incorporating regular breaks, individuals can reduce mental fatigue and maintain a more sustainable level of energy throughout the day. This approach fosters a sense of accomplishment after completing each Pomodoro, contributing to improved mental well-being.

3. Eat That Frog!

Popularized by Brian Tracy in his book *Eat That Frog!*, this approach suggests prioritizing the most difficult or crucial task as the initial activity of the day. The concept originates from the notion that if you start each morning by consuming a live frog, you can navigate the rest of the day with the reassurance that you've already faced the most challenging obstacle.

By addressing the most daunting task early on, individuals can avoid procrastination and the stress that accompanies delaying important responsibilities. This technique helps set a positive tone for the day, fostering a sense of accomplishment and reducing the mental burden associated with procrastination.

4. Time Blocking

By implementing time blocking, you can schedule distinct time blocks for various activities throughout your day. This method enables you to set aside dedicated time for work, personal tasks, and breaks, establishing a structured and

organized routine. By visually mapping out how you spend your time, you can pinpoint potential time-wasters and fine-tune your schedule to enhance productivity.

To implement effective time blocking, individuals should identify their most productive periods and assign tasks accordingly. Establishing clear boundaries between your work and personal time helps you prevent the spillover of stressors from one domain to another. It also provides a sense of control over one's schedule, contributing to improved mental well-being.

5. ABCDE Method

The ABCDE method, introduced by Alan Lakein, involves categorizing tasks based on their importance and the consequences of not completing them. Tasks are assigned letters: A for highly important, B for less important, C for tasks with no significant consequences, D for tasks that can be delegated, and E for tasks that can be eliminated.

By applying the ABCDE method to prioritize tasks systematically, you can direct your energy toward what truly matters. This method promotes a proactive mindset, helping you avoid the buildup of stress resulting from neglecting essential responsibilities. Keeping a routine review and update of task priorities ensures that you stay in sync with your goals, minimizing the chances of feeling overwhelmed.

Tips for Effective Time Management

- Establish clear, achievable goals for effective time management.
- Define short-term and long-term objectives to guide daily tasks.
- Prioritize using tools like the Eisenhower Matrix, addressing urgent and important tasks first.
- Learn to say no to maintain a manageable workload.
- Utilize technology for task organization, reminders, and progress tracking.
- Regularly review and adjust time management strategies for optimal efficiency.

Decision-Making Techniques

Pros and Cons Analysis

When faced with a decision, utilizing a pros and cons analysis entails creating a simple list outlining the favorable and unfavorable aspects connected to each option being evaluated. This method aids decision-makers in weighing the advantages and disadvantages, providing a clearer under-standing of potential outcomes. For instance, if you're contemplating a job offer, you might list the perks of the new position against potential drawbacks, helping to make an informed choice that aligns with your personal and profes-sional goals.

Decision Matrix

In the decision matrix technique, decision-makers assign weights or importance to different criteria relevant to their

decision. Subsequently, options are evaluated based on these weighted criteria. This structured approach facilitates an objective assessment, considering various factors that matter. When you're making decisions for your business, you might assign weights to factors such as cost, reliability, and product quality, especially when selecting a supplier. The decision matrix then helps in systematically comparing supplier options and making a choice that aligns with the company's priorities.

SWOT Analysis

SWOT analysis involves evaluating the strengths, weaknesses, opportunities, and threats of each option. By examining these aspects, decision-makers gain a comprehensive understanding of the situation. For instance, if you're considering a career change, identifying personal strengths and weaknesses as well as external opportunities and threats in the job market aids in strategic decision-making. Leveraging strengths, addressing weaknesses, and navigating potential challenges become integral parts of the decision-making process.

Decision Trees

Visualizing potential outcomes and decisions in a tree-like structure characterizes decision trees. This technique is particularly beneficial in complex scenarios, helping to map out the different paths choices could lead to. For example, in project management, decision trees can illustrate various project development paths, highlighting potential risks and facilitating better planning for uncertainties.

Six Thinking Hats

The Six Thinking Hats method involves analyzing a decision from six different perspectives, including emotional, logical, and creative angles. This technique encourages a well-rounded evaluation by considering diverse viewpoints. For instance, when deciding on a marketing strategy, each "hat" represents a distinct mode of thinking. This fosters creativity, ensures logical coherence, and acknowledges emotional aspects, resulting in a more comprehensive decision-making process.

Cost-Benefit Analysis

In a cost-benefit analysis, decision-makers evaluate the costs and benefits associated with each decision, often quantifying them. By assigning values to positives and negatives, this technique allows for an objective assessment of whether the benefits outweigh the costs. For instance, in a business that is considering implementing new technology, a cost-benefit analysis would weigh the upfront investment against the anticipated long-term gains in efficiency and revenue.

Helpful Tips

- Clearly state your decision objectives for a guiding framework aligned with your goals.
- Collect pertinent data for informed decisions, ensuring a solid understanding of the situation.
- Explore alternatives to allow a comprehensive evaluation before settling on a decision.
- Employ tools, like pros/cons lists or SWOT analyses, for clarity and organized decision-making.

- Resist impulsivity; take time to weigh options, especially for significant choices.
- Assess potential outcomes to align choices with your risk tolerance.
- Seek input from trusted individuals or experts for valuable insights.
- Project long-term consequences to align decisions with broader objectives.
- Balance rational analysis with emotional awareness during decision-making.
- Ensure decisions align with identified core values for long-term satisfaction.
- Reflect on past choices, extracting lessons to enhance decision-making skills.
- Address smaller components for complex decisions, reducing overwhelm.
- Establish a reasonable time frame to avoid procrastination and stress.

INTERACTIVE ELEMENT

Writing Your Stress Away

Keeping a stress diary or journal can help you manage stress and improve your general well-being. Here's how to get started:

Setting up Your Stress Diary

1. Choose a digital option, such as note-taking software, or a physical diary based on your

preference. Choose the one that is easy to use and fits your preferences.
2. Make time every day for journaling, whether it's in the evening to reflect on your experiences or in the morning to set goals for the day.
3. Locate a quiet, comfortable space where you can express yourself honestly without worrying about being judged.

Helpful Journaling Tips

- Express yourself without thinking about grammar or structure. Let your ideas flow naturally onto the page.
- Adopt an honest stance and write with transparency and sincerity. Being vulnerable encourages sincere introspection and personal development.
- Pay attention to your emotions and bodily sensations. Describe the feelings, ideas, and experiences you associate with your stressors.
- Incorporate moments of gratitude into your journal. Turn your attention away from your worries to the things that are good in your life.
- Periodically revisit previous entries to reflect on patterns, track progress, and identify areas for improvement.

Journal Prompts for Stress Relief

1. Today, I felt stressed when...
2. One thing I can do to alleviate stress is...
3. I am grateful for... because it brings me joy.

4. A stressful situation I handled well today was...
5. My body feels tense when I'm stressed. Today, I noticed tension in...
6. A self-care activity I can engage in to reduce stress is...
7. Three things that bring me peace or comfort are...
8. When I'm stressed, my thoughts tend to...
9. An affirmation I can use to calm my mind is...
10. A challenge I faced today and how I overcame it was...

Starting a stress diary can be a transformative practice in managing stress and developing resilience. By dedicating time to journaling regularly, you empower yourself to explore emotions, identify triggers, and implement effective coping strategies. Remember, your journal is a personal sanctuary for self-discovery and growth, so embrace the journey with openness and compassion toward yourself.

Calm Begins With a "See"

In neuro-linguistic programming (NLP), a potent technique is visualization, where you generate vivid mental images of outcomes or scenarios you desire. It works by harnessing the brain's ability to respond to mental imagery, influencing thoughts, emotions, and behaviors. When you visualize, your brain interprets the imagined scenarios as real experiences, activating similar neural pathways and physiological responses. By repeatedly visualizing positive outcomes, you can reprogram your subconscious mind, leading to reduced stress and anxiety.

To begin using visualization for inner peace, find a quiet and comfortable space where you won't be disturbed. You can close your eyes and engage in several deep breaths to help relax both your body and mind. Then, visualize a serene scene that brings you comfort and tranquility. It could be a peaceful beach, a lush forest, or a serene mountain landscape. Engage all your senses in the visualization: Feel the warmth of the sun, hear the soothing sounds of nature, smell the fresh air, and taste the crispness of the environment.

As you engage with the visualization, concentrate on letting go of any tension or stress within your body. Envision each breath dispelling negativity and imbuing you with a sense of calmness and serenity. Permit yourself to completely embrace the peace and tranquility of the scene, absorbing the positive emotions it brings forth.

It's essential to remind yourself that visualization is a tool for relaxation and self-improvement, not a guarantee of future outcomes. Not everything you visualize will manifest in reality, so it's important to maintain a realistic perspective. Instead, view visualization as a practice for cultivating inner peace and managing stress and anxiety in the present moment.

Incorporating visualization into your daily routine can profoundly enhance overall well-being. Through consistent practice, train your mind to respond positively to challenges, fostering inner peace and resilience against stress and anxiety.

CHAPTER 6
N: NO TIME BUT NOW

If it's out of your hands, it deserves freedom from your mind too.

IVAN NURU

THE PAST AND THE FUTURE... AND OVERTHINKING

Do you find yourself caught in the intricate web of overthinking where your mind incessantly replays past mistakes and projects worries about the uncertain future? You are not alone. Many individuals grapple with the incessant chatter of their own thoughts, creating a mental loop that seems impossible to escape. Two common triggers that fuel this overthinking spiral include ruminating over past mistakes and worrying about the future. Let's explore how these tendencies take root and how breaking free from their grip is not only possible but essential for a healthier mindset.

The Weight of Past Mistakes

Imagine sitting in a quiet room, trying to focus on the present moment when, suddenly, a vivid memory of a past mistake barges in, uninvited. Your mind begins to dissect the event, analyzing every detail and assigning blame. This rumination over past mistakes can be a powerful trigger for overthinking. The "what ifs" and "should haves" become haunting echoes, preventing you from fully engaging with the current moment.

You messed up, your inner critic whispers. *How could you be so foolish?* it chides. The weight of past mistakes becomes a burden, and you find yourself stuck in a cycle of self-blame and regret.

Acknowledging the lessons from past mistakes is crucial, but dwelling on them excessively hinders personal growth. Acknowledging that everyone makes mistakes is crucial; it's an integral aspect of the human journey. Instead of criticizing yourself, utilize these experiences as stepping stones for your own learning and improvement. By reframing your perspective, you can break the chain of past mistakes and allow yourself the freedom to move forward.

The Anxiety of Future Worries

The future is a vast and unknown territory that often triggers anxiety and uncertainty. Thoughts about what might happen, what challenges lie ahead, and whether you are equipped to handle them can consume your mental space. When you continually worry about the future, it can turn into a breeding ground for overthinking.

You're not prepared for what's coming, your inner worrier warns. *What if everything falls apart?* it questions. The anxiety about the future can lead to a state of perpetual stress, hindering your ability to enjoy the present.

It's important to acknowledge that the future is unpredictable, and worrying about it excessively won't change the outcome. Instead of succumbing to the anxiety of what might be, focus on the present moment and the actions you can take today. By channeling your energy into the things you can control, you empower yourself to face the future with resilience and adaptability.

RELEASING RESENTMENT

Forgiveness is a powerful act of self-liberation that helps you to let go of old grudges and resentment, making way for healing and personal progress. Holding onto resentment can be like carrying a huge burden that affects your mental and emotional health. To begin a road of forgiveness, it is critical to recognize the significant influence it can have on your life.

First and foremost, acknowledge the pain. It's okay to be upset and angry at the actions of others. By recognizing these emotions, you give yourself permission to feel and understand the depths of your sentiments. Remember that forgiveness isn't about accepting the actions that brought you pain; rather, it's about breaking free from those bad emotions.

Reflect on the reasons behind your decision to forgive, and consider the toll that holding onto grudges takes on your mental and emotional health. Recognize that forgiveness is a gift you give to yourself, not necessarily to the person who wronged you. When you hold onto resentment, you allow the past to control your present, and by choosing forgiveness, you reclaim your power and control over your own life.

You need empathy to forgive, and this can be done by putting yourself in the shoes of the person who hurt you. This doesn't mean justifying their actions but understanding that everyone is human and susceptible to mistakes. Recognizing their imperfections can humanize them in your eyes and make it easier to let go of resentment. Remember, forgiving someone doesn't mean you have to forget what happened; it means you are choosing not to let it control your emotions.

Practice self-compassion, and understand that you, too, are fallible. Just as you extend forgiveness to others, be willing to forgive yourself for any role you played in the situation. Self-compassion allows you to let go of guilt or shame, fostering an environment where forgiveness can thrive.

Communication can be a valuable element in the forgiveness process. If you feel safe, consider expressing your feelings to the individual who offended you. This does not always require face-to-face confrontation; it can be accomplished through a sincere letter or a mediated talk. Honest conversation can lead to understanding, and sometimes just voicing your feelings can provide a cathartic relief.

Cultivate gratitude for the lessons learned. Every experience, even painful ones, contributes to your personal growth. By focusing on the lessons gained from the situation, you shift your perspective from victimhood to empowerment. Gratitude helps to transform bitterness into an opportunity for self-improvement.

Set healthy boundaries. Forgiveness doesn't necessarily mean allowing someone to repeatedly hurt you rather, establish clear boundaries to protect yourself from further harm. Boundaries are a form of self-respect and demonstrate that you value your well-being.

Finally, make time your ally. Forgiveness is a process, not an immediate solution. Be patient with yourself while navigating your emotional landscape. Healing takes time, and it's fine to have setbacks. Celebrate tiny successes and appreciate your accomplishments along the road.

Situations Where Forgiveness Is Not Possible

Forgiveness is a difficult emotional process, and while it may be a great tool for healing, there are times when it may appear impossible. Extreme betrayal, permanent injury, or repeated wrongdoings can leave deep wounds that are beyond forgiving. In circumstances of horrific crimes, such as extreme acts of violence or abuse, the victim may find it impossible to forgive the perpetrator.

Additionally, systemic or institutional injustices where an individual or group is oppressed over an extended period can present challenges to forgiveness. For instance, if you have been subjected to systemic discrimination or oppression, forgiving the entire system or those perpetuating it may be difficult due to ongoing harm and lack of accountability.

Personal boundaries are crucial in determining the feasibility of forgiveness. If someone continuously demonstrates a lack of remorse or persists in harmful behavior, forgiveness may be unattainable. For example, forgiving an unrepentant and manipulative individual who consistently betrays your trust might be unrealistic, as it may perpetuate a cycle of harm.

Ultimately, forgiveness is a deeply personal and nuanced process influenced by the severity of the transgression, the acknowledgment of wrongdoing, and the capacity for meaningful change.

ACCEPTING UNCERTAINTY

Life is full of twists, turns, and unforeseen detours. One of the most difficult things about this journey is the uncertainty that surrounds it. From career choices to personal relationships, the unpredictability of the future can be a significant source of stress for many individuals.

Uncertainty is an unavoidable aspect of the human experience. Even if we prepare methodically, there will always be elements beyond our control. It is critical to grasp that the pursuit of ultimate certainty is a delusion, like a mirage in the desert of life. Accepting this reality is the first step toward facing uncertainty.

- **Shift Your Perspective**

Instead of viewing uncertainty as a threat, consider it as an opportunity for growth and discovery. Life's unpredictability often leads to unexpected opportunities, new relationships, and personal development. Think of uncertainty as a blank canvas waiting for you to paint your unique masterpiece. For example, imagine you're facing a career crossroads. Instead of fearing the unknown, see it as a chance to explore different paths and uncover hidden talents.

- **Lean on Support Systems**

Navigating uncertainty is easier when you have a strong support system. Share your concerns with friends, family, or a trusted confidant. Sometimes, voicing your fears and uncertainties can provide relief and open the door to valuable insights and perspectives. Consider someone going through a challenging personal situation—confiding in a friend can offer emotional support and perhaps even lead to practical solutions.

- **Foster Resilience**

Developing resilience is necessary for managing uncertainty. People who are resilient can overcome obstacles, recover from failures, and prosper in the face of uncertainty. Develop a positive mindset, learn lessons from your mistakes, and find purpose in the obstacles you face in order to build resilience. Consider the analogy of a tree bending with the wind but not breaking. In a similar vein, resilience allows you to withstand uncertainty without losing your fundamental strength.

- **Set Realistic Expectations**

Uncertainty often arises from unmet expectations and the fear of the unknown. Manage your expectations by understanding that not everything in life can be planned or controlled. Setting realistic expectations allows you to adapt more easily when faced with unforeseen circumstances. For example, in a romantic relationship, instead of expecting perfection, acknowledge that challenges will arise and that both partners will need to navigate them together.

- **Embrace Flexibility**

Flexibility is essential while dealing with uncertainty. Rigidity can exacerbate stress, whereas flexibility enables adaptation to changing conditions. Consider a professional facing a rapid change in their field; individuals who accept flexibility are more likely to pivot successfully and pursue new chances. Adapting empowers you to leverage uncertainty for personal and professional growth.

As you grow through life, remember that the journey is just as important as the destination, and uncertainty is a constant companion on this remarkable adventure called life.

ACCEPTING REALITY AS IT IS

Life is an unpredictable journey that often throws unexpected challenges our way. At times, we find ourselves facing situations that are beyond our control, leaving us grappling with frustration and a sense of powerlessness. However, in the face of adversity, it is essential to develop the ability to come to terms with things we cannot change. By identifying the silver lining, focusing on what we can control, pursuing community, and striving to improve conditions for others, we can navigate these challenges with resilience and find a sense of peace.

Firstly, identifying the silver lining in seemingly dire situations is a powerful way to shift your perspective. While it may initially be difficult, reframing the narrative around a challenging circumstance can open up new possibilities for your growth. For instance, consider yourself in a situation where you lose your job unexpectedly. Instead of dwelling on the negative aspects, you might focus on the opportunity to explore new career paths, acquire new skills, or spend more time with your loved ones. By searching for the positive aspects in any situation, you are empowering yourself to adapt and find a sense of meaning amid the chaos.

Secondly, focusing on what you can control is a fundamental principle in managing the unchangeable. Life's uncertainties can be overwhelming, but directing your energy toward aspects within your control can provide a sense of agency. For example, if facing a health issue, concentrate on adopting a healthier lifestyle through diet and exercise. By taking charge of manageable elements in your life, you create a foundation for stability and personal well-being, even when larger circumstances may remain beyond your influence.

Furthermore, seeking community is an important part of coming to grips with the unchangeable. Connecting with people who have had similar experiences or can provide support can be really comforting. This shared knowledge instills a sense of belonging and reminds you that you are not alone in overcoming obstacles. Consider the example of a person dealing with the loss of a loved one. Joining a support group or engaging with friends who have gone through similar experiences can provide a network of understanding and empathy, making the burden more bearable.

Finally, actively seeking to better the conditions of others is an effective method to direct your energy productively. While you may be unable to change your personal circumstances, helping others can provide a feeling of purpose and joy. Take the example of someone who is physically limited due to a chronic illness. They may channel their efforts into volunteering for a cause they are passionate about or advocating for better accessibility for people with disabilities. By making a positive impact on the lives of others, you not only contribute to the greater good but also find a sense of accomplishment and purpose beyond your personal challenges.

FOCUS ON WHAT YOU CAN AND CANNOT DO

In the tumultuous sea of life, one skill that can serve as a guiding light is the ability to concentrate on what's within your control. The ancient Stoics—philosophers who thrived in the turbulence of their times—often emphasized the importance of distinguishing between things within and beyond one's control.

Firstly, let's consider the realms of control. Picture a circle, and within it, place all the elements over which you have a direct influence. These are the aspects of your life where your choices, actions, and reactions hold sway. For instance, your attitudes, behaviors, and decisions are within this circle.

You can control how you respond to events, your work ethic, and the way you treat others.

Now, outside this circle lies the vast expanse of factors beyond your direct control. These may include external events, other people's opinions, and even unpredictable twists of fate. Recognizing this distinction is crucial for maintaining focus. You cannot control the weather, the traffic, or the global economy; however, you can control how you prepare for unforeseen circumstances, manage your time, and adapt to changes.

By adopting a proactive approach and concentrating on what's within your control, you can enhance your focus, productivity, and overall well-being. Here are five strategies you can follow.

- **Be Real With Yourself**

By acknowledging personal strengths, weaknesses, and triggers, individuals can develop strategies to manage their reactions effectively. For example, suppose you tend to get overwhelmed when facing tight deadlines. In that case, being real with yourself involves recognizing this pattern and implementing techniques like breaking tasks into smaller, more manageable steps or practicing mindfulness to stay focused.

- **Get Rid of Crutch Words**

Crutch words, such as "like," "um," or "you know," can signal uncertainty and distract both the speaker and the listener. Imagine you are giving a presentation at work, and you constantly use filler words. Getting rid of these crutch words not only enhances your message's clarity but also strengthens your concentration as you become more mindful of your speech patterns.

- **Reclaim Control of the Schedule**

Creating a well-organized schedule enables people to allocate their time wisely and prioritize responsibilities. Consider a situation in which your daily routine seems chaotic and unpredictable. Taking charge of your schedule entails creating realistic goals, breaking them down into doable steps, and allocating particular time intervals for concentrated effort. This systematic method reduces the feeling of being overwhelmed and encourages prolonged concentration.

- **Start Working on Self-Love**

When individuals feel confident and secure in themselves, they are better equipped to concentrate on tasks without being bogged down by self-doubt. For instance, if you constantly question your abilities and worth, practicing self-love involves acknowledging your accomplishments, learning from mistakes, and embracing your unique qualities. This newfound self-assurance becomes a powerful foundation for sustained concentration.

- **Be Okay With Not Knowing**

In a world where information is abundant yet ever-changing, it's crucial to recognize that not everything can be known or controlled. Suppose you're grappling with the uncertainty of a career decision. Being okay with not knowing involves acknowledging that you cannot predict every outcome, embracing the learning process, and focusing on making informed decisions within your control.

LIVING IN THE MOMENT

It's easy to find ourselves caught up in the chaos of tomorrow or the regrets of yesterday, leaving little room for the beauty of the present moment. However, the key to a more fulfilling and joyful life lies in our ability to be fully present. By cultivating mindfulness and incorporating simple practices into your daily routine, you can unlock the power of *now* and savor the richness of each moment. Here are 10 principles to help you navigate the path of mindfulness and fully experience the richness of each moment in your life.

- **Remove Unneeded Possessions**

Imagine your living space cluttered with items that carry the weight of past memories. Minimalism advocates for shedding unnecessary possessions, liberating you from the shackles of the past. By letting go of objects associated with memories, you create space for the present. For example, donating old clothes can symbolize a fresh start, allowing you to appreciate the current phase of your life.

- **Smile**

A simple smile can transform your outlook on the day. You possess the power to control your attitude each morning. By starting the day with optimism, you set the tone for the hours ahead. Cultivate a habit of intentional smiling, and soon, it will become a reflex, influencing your interactions and experiences positively.

- **Fully Appreciate the Moments of Today**

Life unfolds in a series of moments, each offering a unique blend of sights, sounds, and emotions. To truly live in the moment, actively engage with your surroundings. Whether it's relishing the aroma of fresh coffee in the morning or appreciating the beauty of a sunset, savor the details that make each day special.

- **Forgive Past Grievances**

Harboring resentment toward others for past grievances can anchor you in the past. Choose to forgive and release the burden of past pain. By doing so, you reclaim control over your present mood and allow yourself to be fully present. For instance, forgiving a friend for a past disagreement enables you to enjoy your current time together without the shadow of the past.

- **Dream About the Future But Work Hard Today**

Balancing dreams for the future with present action is key. While it's crucial to set goals and envision a brighter tomorrow, the foundation for those dreams is laid in the actions of today. For example, if you dream of starting your own business, taking small steps like researching the industry or networking can bring you closer to that goal.

- **Don't Dwell on Past Accomplishments**

Reflecting on past achievements is valuable, but dwelling on them can hinder present growth. Instead, focus on building upon past successes. Consider someone who achieved a fitness milestone last year—the key is not to dwell on that accomplishment but to continue the fitness journey and create new memories and achievements.

- **Stop Worrying**

Worrying about tomorrow detracts from fully appreciating today. Acknowledge that tomorrow will arrive regardless of your concerns. Redirect mental energy away from worry, allowing yourself to be more present in the current moment.

- **Think Beyond Old Solutions to Problems**

Adapting to a changing world requires a mindset open to new solutions. Avoid clinging to outdated approaches, and be willing to explore fresh perspectives. For example, in the workplace, embracing innovative solutions rather than relying on traditional methods can lead to increased efficiency and success.

- **Conquer Addictions**

Addictions can chain you to the past or pull you away from the present. Overcoming addictions, whether they be related to substances, technology, or other behaviors, liberates you to fully engage with the current moment. Seeking professional help or joining support groups are steps toward living addiction-free and in the moment.

INTERACTIVE ELEMENT

Ready... Set... Let Go!

1. Think back to a recent setback or disappointment. How can you rephrase it to present it from a more optimistic angle?
2. What self-limiting ideas do you have about who you are? How can you use empowering affirmations in their place?
3. List three things you are thankful for today, no matter how little. How can you extend your thankfulness into tomorrow?
4. Tell about a time when you were genuinely happy and at peace. What components helped create that atmosphere, and how can you replicate them?
5. Compose a letter of forgiveness and compassion to your former self. How would you advise the younger version of yourself?
6. To gain more inner peace, make a list of the three things you need to let go of. How do you begin letting them go?

7. Look into a fun pastime or activity that you enjoy. How can you bring this into your everyday life more?

8. Write about a dream or objective that you've been afraid to go after. What little actions may you take to get in that direction?

9. What unfavorable mental patterns or behaviors are preventing you from achieving your dream? How can you swap them out for beneficial ones?

10. Consider a relationship that might require mending. What steps can you take to repair and enhance that relationship?

11. Give an example of a time when you were fully present and conscious. How can your daily routine include greater mindfulness?

12. Make a list of the things that stress you out or sap your energy. How can these sources be reduced or eliminated?

13. Examine your worries and fears. What actions can you take to confront and get past them?

14. Write about a recent success, regardless of its size. In what ways can you work to acknowledge your accomplishments more frequently?

15. Think about those who inspire and motivate you. How can you intentionally surround yourself with uplifting individuals?

In conclusion, this chapter encourages us to break free from the chains of resentment, navigate uncertainty with grace, and relish the beauty of the present moment. By incorporating the lessons within, we can embark on a journey toward mental liberation and a more fulfilling life. In the next chapter, we will gain guidance on what habits we can practice that will help with our anxiety and overthinking.

CHAPTER 7
ZEN-SIBLE HABITS FOR
A DECLUTTERED MIND

We cannot become what we want by remaining what we are.

MAX DEPREE

GET ENOUGH SLEEP

I t's easy to overlook one of the most powerful tools for maintaining mental health: sleep. Yet, beneath the veil of night, as you drift into slumber, your brain sets on a journey of restoration and rejuvenation that can significantly impact your anxiety levels and overall well-being. Seriously, it's like your own personal therapist that you don't even have to book an appointment with! Here's the lowdown in a way that might just make you want to cozy up for an early night.

First off, picture this: You're running on four hours of sleep; your brain feels like it's wading through mud, and every little thing seems to set off a mini panic attack. Sound familiar?

That's your brain telling you it needs a serious recharge. When you're sleep-deprived, it's like your anxiety gets cranked up to 11. It's harder to concentrate, emotions run wild, and that sense of dread lurks in the background. It's practically throwing a party in your mind. The emotional centers of your brain become hyperactive, amplifying feelings of stress and anxiety.

But here comes sleep to the rescue! When you give your brain the rest it deserves, magical things happen. During sleep, your brain sorts through all the chaos of the day, filing away memories, processing emotions, and basically hitting the reset button. It's like overnight therapy, minus the awkward silences.

Ever noticed how, after a solid night's sleep, things just seem more manageable? That's because sleep helps regulate your emotions. It's like armor against the onslaught of anxiety-inducing thoughts. You wake up feeling more grounded and capable of handling whatever life decides to throw your way.

Think of sleep as your body's natural antidepressant, flooding your brain with feel-good chemicals like serotonin and dopamine while taming the runaway stress hormone, cortisol. As you bask in the tranquility of deep sleep, your brain orchestrates a symphony of neurotransmitters, promoting a sense of calm and serenity that can shield you from the storm of anxiety.

And let's not forget about the physical benefits of sleep. Your body needs that downtime to repair and rejuvenate. When you're well-rested, you're more likely to have the energy to tackle the day, whether it's facing that big presentation at work or just dealing with the usual chaos of life.

Moreover, sleep is important for cognitive function, which sharpens your mental acuity and bolsters your ability to cope with life's challenges. When you're well rested, your mind becomes a fortress, better equipped to fend off negative thoughts and intrusive worries. With each sleep cycle, your brain engages in a process of memory consolidation, storing away essential information while discarding the mental clutter that weighs you down.

But the benefits of sleep extend far beyond the confines of your mind, permeating every facet of your being. A restorative night's sleep strengthens your immune system, fortifying your body against the physical toll of stress and anxiety. It nourishes your cardiovascular health, lowering your risk of heart disease and hypertension. It even enhances your metabolism, helping you maintain a healthy weight and ward off mood-disrupting fluctuations in your blood sugar.

Making sleep a priority isn't just about catching z's; it's an act of self-care. It's saying to yourself, "Hey, I deserve this." And you do! You deserve to wake up feeling refreshed, ready to take on whatever the day throws at you. So tonight, do yourself a favor: Tuck yourself in a little earlier, snuggle up with your favorite pillow, and let sleep work its magic. Your mind—and your sanity—will thank you for it.

Sleep Tips

Incorporating the following personalized sleep tips can improve your nightly rest and morning energy. Quality sleep is vital for a healthy, fulfilling life; prioritize it for better physical and mental well-being.

Ensuring you sleep well is vital for your overall well-being. By embracing healthy sleep habits, you can significantly enhance your rest quality. Here are personalized tips to optimize your sleep routine, ensuring you wake up refreshed each morning.

- Investing in a better mattress and bedding is an investment in your sleep quality. Think about it— you spend about a third of your life in bed, so make it count. Evaluate your mattress regularly to ensure it provides adequate support and comfort. Your bedding should also be cozy and inviting, promoting a relaxing sleep environment.
- Blocking out light is crucial for signaling to your body that it's time to sleep. You can improve your bedroom environment by investing in blackout curtains or an eye mask, creating a dark and serene atmosphere. This straightforward change can greatly improve your ability to both fall asleep and stay asleep.
- Minimize noise to improve your sleep. To create a peaceful sleeping environment, block out distracting noises with earplugs or white noise generators.
- By consistently setting your alarm for the same time every day, including weekends, you are helping your body regulate its internal clock. This regularity reinforces your natural sleep-wake cycle, facilitating easier transitions into sleep at night and waking up in the morning with a revitalized feeling.
- Disconnect from screens an hour before bed as blue light disrupts melatonin, hindering sleep. Instead, relax with a book, bath, or calming activities.

- By dedicating 30 minutes before bedtime to relaxation, you signal to your body that it's time to unwind. Engage in calming activities such as gentle stretching, meditation, or deep breathing to prepare your mind and body for a restful night's sleep.
- Regular exercise, at least 20 minutes each day, contributes to better sleep. Engaging in physical activity supports relaxation and contributes to the regulation of your sleep patterns. Nevertheless, it's advisable to steer clear of vigorous workouts near bedtime, as they might have a counterproductive impact on your sleep.
- Limit caffeine after 2 p.m. to avoid sleep disruption. Be aware of hidden caffeine in medications and chocolate; choose decaf in the afternoon and evening.
- Alcohol may induce initial drowsiness but disrupts later sleep cycles. Finish alcoholic drinks at least an hour before bedtime for proper alcohol metabolism.
- Maintaining a sleep diary aids in recognizing patterns and highlighting areas for enhancing your sleep routine. Record your sleep schedule, daily activities, and factors influencing your sleep, and use this data to adjust habits and improve sleep quality.

CONSIDER YOUR DIET

Did you know that what you eat doesn't just impact your body but your mind too? It's like a secret connection between your plate and your mood. Let's dive into why your diet plays a major role in your mental well-being.

Think of your brain as a high-performance car; to keep it running smoothly, you need to fuel it with the good stuff. You can think of nutrient-rich foods such as fruits, vegetables, whole grains, and lean proteins as high-quality fuel for your brain. These foods supply the vitamins, minerals, and antioxidants that your brain requires to operate at its optimal level.

But just like putting cheap gas in your car can make it sputter and stall, loading up on junk food can throw your brain into a funk. Foods high in sugar, saturated fats, and processed ingredients might give you a temporary boost, but they can also lead to mood swings, fatigue, and even long-term mental health issues like anxiety and depression.

Ever heard of serotonin? It's a neurotransmitter that controls mood and sleep patterns. Guess what helps your body produce more serotonin? Yep, you guessed it—certain foods! Eating foods rich in tryptophan, like turkey, nuts, and seeds, can give your serotonin levels a natural boost, leaving you feeling happier and more relaxed.

Your gut is like the control center for your mood. When your gut is happy, chances are, you are too. Consuming a fiber and probiotic-rich diet fosters a healthy gut microbiome, potentially lowering inflammation and enhancing mood.

So, the next time you're feeling stressed or down, take a look at what's on your plate. Making small changes to your diet— like swapping out sugary snacks for fresh fruit or adding more leafy greens to your meals—can make a big difference in how you feel. After all, you wouldn't put low-grade fuel in a Ferrari, would you? Treat your brain like the high-performance machine it is, and feed it the good stuff it deserves.

Anti-Anxiety Diet

When it comes to managing anxiety through your diet, some foods can be your best buddies and others might be good to avoid. Here's the lowdown on what to eat and what to avoid to help reduce those anxious feelings:

What to Eat

1. **Fatty Fish:** Sardines, mackerel, and salmon are great options. These fish species are high in omega-3 fatty acids, which are well-known for their capacity to reduce anxiety and promote mental health.
2. **Complex Carbs:** Make whole grains like brown rice, quinoa, and oats your pals. They lessen the emotional fluctuations that worry can bring on by stabilizing blood sugar levels.
3. **Leafy Greens:** You can eat kale, spinach, and Swiss chard—they're rich in magnesium, which plays a key role in regulating mood and reducing anxiety.
4. **Probiotics:** Support gut health by adding yogurt, kefir, and sauerkraut to your diet. Probiotics aid in fostering a balanced gut microbiome, linked to lower anxiety levels.
5. **Nuts and Seeds:** Packed with healthy fats, vitamins, and minerals to promote mental well-being and reduce anxiety, almonds, walnuts, and flaxseeds offer various nutrient-dense options.
6. **Lean Proteins:** Chicken, turkey, and tofu are protein sources that help stabilize blood sugar levels and keep you feeling full and satisfied, which can help reduce anxiety.

What to Avoid

1. **Caffeine Overload:** While that morning cup of coffee is a ritual for many, too much caffeine can amp up anxiety. Keep an eye on your intake and maybe consider decaf in the afternoon.
2. **Sugar Rush and Crash:** Sweets and sugary treats might give you a momentary high, but the crash afterward can leave you feeling irritable and anxious. Opt for natural sugars in fruits instead.
3. **Alcohol:** While alcohol may offer temporary stress relief, it's crucial to recognize it as a depressant that can exacerbate anxiety over time. Optimal well-being hinges on moderation.
4. **Processed Foods:** Those bags of chips and fast food burgers may be convenient, but the additives and preservatives can mess with your mood. Opt for fresh, whole foods instead.
5. **Excessive Salt:** High sodium levels can mess with your blood pressure and contribute to feelings of anxiety. Keep an eye on your salt intake and opt for herbs and spices for flavor.

Remember, it's not about drastic changes overnight. Small, consistent tweaks to your diet can make a big impact over time. And always, listen to your body—it's your best guide on this journey to a calmer, happier you.

EXERCISE

Exercise is a potent remedy for anxiety, effectively tackling worries head-on. Instead of remaining ensnared in anxious feelings, picture putting on your sneakers and opting for a walk or run when you feel jittery and tense. Physical activity functions like a magical elixir for your brain, releasing chemicals that generate a sense of well-being.

Engaging in exercise prompts the production of endorphins, acting as natural mood enhancers and pain relievers. These neurotransmitters flood your brain with positive feelings, creating a warm and reassuring sensation, signaling that everything will be okay.

In addition to the immediate endorphin boost, physical activity also diminishes cortisol levels—the stress hormone. That tight feeling in your chest during anxious moments? That's cortisol in action. Yet, movement actively expels excess cortisol, leaving you with a lighter and more relaxed feeling.

As a valuable extra, regular exercise can reshape your brain over time, reducing its susceptibility to stress and anxiety. This process is comparable to constructing a mental shield against persistent worries, bolstering your resilience and capacity to navigate life's challenges.

The key is to find an activity you enjoy and make it a consistent part of your routine. So, the next time anxiety strikes, don't just sit there—get up, get moving, and let those feel-good endorphins do their magic.

Relaxing Routines

Integrating the following listed exercises into your daily routine offers a comprehensive strategy for addressing both physical and mental well-being, taking into account individual preferences and requirements. Identifying activities that bring about happiness and satisfaction is crucial for promoting overall health.

- **Running**

Running is a multifaceted activity beneficial for mental health. It initiates the release of endorphins, commonly referred to as "feel-good" hormones, which effectively diminish stress and anxiety levels. Regular running is associated with mood enhancement and can alleviate symptoms in individuals coping with depression. Moreover, running doubles as a form of mindfulness, enabling individuals to concentrate on the present moment and clear their minds during this invigorating exercise.

- **Yoga**

Yoga offers a comprehensive approach to mental well-being through various mechanisms. It integrates stress relief techniques, including breathing exercises and meditation, fostering relaxation and reducing stress levels. Beyond the physical aspects, yoga cultivates a strong mind-body connection, promoting self-awareness and mindfulness. The practice has demonstrated efficacy in decreasing symptoms of anxiety, contributing to an overall improvement in mental health.

Activity: Yoga Poses for Stress and Anxiety

1. Mountain Pose (Tadasana)

Stand confidently tall with your feet together or hip-width apart, ensuring an even distribution of weight. Engage your thighs, lift your chest, and roll your shoulders back. As you inhale deeply, extend your arms overhead with your palms facing each other. Hold the pose, feeling strength and stability from head to toe. Breathe deeply.

2. Downward Facing Dog (Adho Mukha Svanasana)

Start by positioning yourself on your hands and knees, ensuring that your wrists are aligned under your shoulders and your knees under your hips. Tuck your toes, lift your hips toward the ceiling, straighten your legs, and let your head hang, creating an inverted "V" shape. Press through palms and heels, elongating your spine. Feel your hamstring stretch, and allow your shoulders to release their tension. Breathe deeply, savoring the stretch.

3. Warrior II (Virabhadrasana II)

Start by standing; step one foot back and bend your front knee. Extend your arms parallel to the floor with your palms facing down. Align your gaze with your front hand as you position it in line with your front knee. Ground through the outer edge of the back foot, feeling strength in your leg. Warrior II opens hips and builds endurance, so breathe deeply and embrace your inner warrior!

4. Tree Pose (Vrikshasana)

Shift your weight to one leg, raising the opposite foot and resting the sole of the foot against your inner thigh or calf (avoiding the knee). Bring your palms together in front or extend your arms overhead. Focus on a point to aid balance and center your mind. Sense stability in your standing leg and breathe to find equilibrium.

5. Child's Pose (Balasana)

To initiate Child's Pose, start by kneeling on your yoga mat and sitting back on your heels. Extend your arms forward, then lower your upper body between your thighs, allowing your forehead to rest on the mat. You can choose to reach your arms further or let them rest alongside your body. Take deep breaths, noticing a subtle stretch in your back and shoulders. Remain in this soothing pose, embracing relaxation and peace.

There you have it, a mini yoga sequence to nurture your body and mind. Enjoy the journey of each pose, and remember, it's about the process, not perfection.

- **Hiking**

Hiking provides a therapeutic experience for the mind by immersing individuals in nature. This exposure has a calming effect, diminishing feelings of anxiety and promoting relaxation. Furthermore, hiking has been linked to increased creativity, potentially attributable to the combination of physical activity and the inspiring surroundings of the natural environment.

- **Weightlifting**

Weightlifting contributes to mental well-being through distinct pathways. Similar to running, it prompts the release of endorphins, fostering an improved mood and stress reduction. Additionally, engaging in regular weightlifting has been correlated with better sleep quality, which is a crucial factor in supporting overall mental health.

- **Taking Long Walks**

Taking long walks emerges as a mindful practice, aligning with the stress-reducing benefits of running and hiking. This deliberate movement provides individuals with an opportunity to clear their minds and alleviate stress. Moreover, the social aspect of walking, especially when done with friends or in a group, facilitates social interaction, contributing positively to mental health.

- **Swimming**

Swimming is recognized as a therapeutic activity for promoting mental well-being. The rhythmic and repetitive aspects of swimming create a meditative impact, fostering relaxation and stress reduction. Furthermore, as swimming involves the activation of diverse muscle groups, it contributes to physical relaxation and the release of tension, amplifying its positive effects on mental health.

- **Dancing**

Dancing, beyond being a physical activity, serves as an expressive outlet for emotions and stress. It enables individuals to convey feelings through movement, acting as a potent form of self-expression. Group or partner dancing not only builds social connections but also improves communication skills. The shared rhythmic experience fosters a sense of unity, promoting teamwork and coordination. Beyond its physical benefits, dancing is a holistic and enjoyable path to emotional well-being, providing a dynamic avenue for self-discovery and connection with others.

BE ONE WITH NATURE

When you immerse yourself in nature, you discover that it has a remarkable ability to heal, soothe, and restore your mental well-being. Mathew White's study emphasizes the abundant cognitive benefits and happiness that come from exposure to nature, revealing how nature therapy can effectively calm depression, improve sleep, and encourage vital social interactions for better mental health ("Nature Therapy: The Benefits of Nature for Mental Health," 2021).

- **Enhanced Cognitive Function**

Spending even a few minutes in nature improves your cognitive function. Cognitive functions encompass intellectual activity, thinking processes, reasoning, and the capacity for memory. A fascinating experiment demonstrates that spending time in nature, even for just a brief period, positively impacts cognitive function, irrespective of an individual's age.

In an intriguing study, a group of students was assigned a demanding task, with one half exposed to a rooftop view and the other to a view of grasses and flowers outside the window. Notably, the students overlooking the garden made fewer errors compared to their counterparts with a rooftop view ("Nature Therapy: The Benefits of Nature for Mental Health," 2021).

The findings from the research suggest that exposure to nature can enhance cognitive function by:

1. Improving concentration levels
2. Enhancing attentional capabilities
3. Reducing stress levels
4. Contributing to a sense of contentment in a fatigued brain
5. Fostering an increased inclination to spend more time in natural surroundings.

- **Calming Effects**

Nature's beauty and serenity have a profound calming effect on your mind, bringing peace that urban spaces often lack. Unlike indoor activities, a nature trip reduces stress, prevents mental fatigue, recharges your mind, and uplifts your mood. Whether at the beach or on a nature hike, the difference in calming your mind is significant. Choosing nature over indoor activities cultivates a positive mindset, helping you tackle challenges with renewed vigor.

- **Improved Overall Well-Being**

Nature's healing effects extend to both mental health and physical well-being. Activities like hiking not only reduce stress and anger but also contribute to physical fitness by regulating blood pressure, muscle tension, and heart rate. Nature therapy becomes a powerful tool for maintaining good health and promoting mindfulness, gratitude, and healthy physical activity, which are essential for a healthier and happier life.

- **Natural Antidepressant**

Spending at least two hours a week in nature calms depression and serves as a preventive measure for depressive symptoms. Nature therapy facilitates mindfulness and gratitude, clearing your mind of unnecessary worries, anxiety, anger, and tension. The combination of nature therapy's mood-boosting impact and exercise's positive effects makes it an effective strategy against obesity, diabetes, high blood pressure, and depression.

- **Improved Social Interactions**

Engaging in nature therapy provides personal benefits and enhances social interactions. Exploring nature alone is beneficial, but bringing along friends makes the experience more enjoyable. Nature trips create opportunities for fun and socializing, leading to the formation of new friendships. This social exposure helps avoid feelings of isolation and loneliness, positively impacting mental health. Choosing to explore nature with others enriches your life and contributes to the collective well-being of your social circle. After all, the joy of nature is best when shared with friends. By choosing nature therapy, you not only take care of your mental well-being but also create avenues for meaningful social connections.

Tips on How to Get Outside More

- Begin your day with a refreshing morning walk—for example, in your neighborhood or a nearby park—ensuring exposure to early sunlight.
- Take your workout routine outside by choosing a local park over the gym. Jog, practice yoga, or engage in bodyweight exercises while enjoying the sun.
- Choose outdoor locations for lunch to benefit from both nourishment and natural sunlight. Find a sunny spot to savor your meal.
- Integrate brief nature breaks into your daily schedule, whether it's a short walk in a nearby green area or simply sitting in a garden to rejuvenate your mind.
- Develop outdoor hobbies like gardening, bird watching, or photography, providing opportunities to connect with nature.
- Plan weekend retreats to natural settings such as hiking trails, beaches, or camping spots for a refreshing immersion in the great outdoors.
- Schedule moments to witness the sunrise or sunset, creating a serene and beautiful connection with nature that promotes a sense of calm.
- Opt for walking meetings instead of indoor sit-downs to incorporate physical activity and enjoy the

outdoor surroundings.

Unplug

In this digital era, taking a moment to unplug from the constant buzz of technology is not just a luxury but a necessity for your well-being. When you deliberately detach yourself from screens and notifications, you embark on a journey to recharge both your mind and body, experiencing a myriad of benefits that significantly reduce stress.

Firstly, by unplugging, you liberate yourself from the relentless stream of information and demands that bombard you daily. Constant connectivity can lead to information overload, leaving you mentally fatigued and overwhelmed. Picture this: You decide to spend an evening without screens, opting for a leisurely walk in a nearby park or indulging in a good book. Without persistent notifications and digital distractions, you create a mental sanctuary, allowing your mind to unwind and find serenity.

Furthermore, consistently exposing yourself to screens, especially before bedtime, interferes with your sleep patterns. When you unplug, you prioritize quality sleep, enhancing your overall well-being. Imagine swapping scrolling through social media before bed for a peaceful evening routine that includes reading a book or practicing relaxation techniques. The result? You wake up feeling refreshed with reduced stress levels and increased mental clarity.

Unplugging also fosters meaningful human connections. In a world dominated by virtual communication, the art of face-to-face interaction is often neglected. When you decide to put away your devices during social gatherings, you open the door to more authentic connections. For instance, instead of capturing every moment on your phone during a dinner with friends, you engage in heartfelt conversations, strengthening your social bonds and creating lasting memories.

Moreover, continual exposure to the carefully manicured lives of others via social media might cause stress and anxiety. Unplugging gives you back command of your story. Imagine spending a weekend appreciating real-life events and avoiding social media. You enjoy the small pleasures of life in the here and now, free from the need to share your existence on the internet.

Unplugging is not just a break from technology; it's a rejuvenating retreat for your mind and soul. By prioritizing moments of disconnection, you invite peace, quality sleep, genuine connections, and a sense of authenticity into your life, creating a harmonious balance that significantly reduces stress. So, the next time you feel the weight of digital demands, consider the liberating power of unplugging to truly recharge your mind.

How to Lessen Your Screen Time

- Set specific daily time constraints for screen usage, and adhere to them diligently. Create designated screen-free areas within your living space, such as the bedroom, to enhance the quality of your sleep.
- Infuse brief screen breaks into your daily routine. Participate in activities like taking a brisk walk,

reading a tangible book, or practicing mindfulness to rejuvenate your mind.

- Prioritize in-person interactions whenever feasible. Opt for face-to-face conversations, favoring phone calls or physical meetings over excessive reliance on messaging applications and social media.
- Allocate specific days or weekends for a digital detox. Disconnect from all screens during these periods to establish a more profound connection with the tangible world and to lessen dependence on technology.
- Leverage the built-in features on your devices to establish daily limits for individual apps. This tool assists in monitoring and managing the time dedicated to social media and other digital platforms.
- Rediscover offline hobbies and interests that don't involve screens. Whether it involves gardening, painting, or playing a musical instrument, engage in activities that capture your focus away from technology.
- Forge morning and bedtime routines that exclude screen involvement. Incorporate activities like journaling, stretching, or savoring a cup of tea to commence and conclude your day without digital distractions.
- Practice mindful screen use. Define specific tasks and time limits for online activities, steering clear of aimless scrolling. This intentional approach facilitates a harmonious balance between digital engagement and real-life experiences.

Go on a Social Media Detox

Taking a social media detox can be a transformative experience for your well-being. Let's break down the step-by-step process to guide you through your first social media detox.

- **Tell People**

This initial step involves informing the people you interact with the most about your decision to go offline temporarily. This serves a dual purpose. Firstly, it holds you accountable; knowing that others are aware of your intentions can deter you from impulsively returning to social media. Secondly, it prevents misunderstandings, as those close to you won't wonder about your sudden online absence. If you manage to stick with the detox, most people won't mind, and some may not even notice the change.

- **Remove Apps and Restrict Access to Websites**

To ensure a successful social media detox, it's crucial to remove the social media apps from your mobile devices, particularly your phone. This step is non-negotiable, as keeping the apps may tempt you to check them sporadically, undermining the purpose of the detox. If going completely offline seems challenging, consider a shorter detox period. Additionally, blocking social media websites on your computer using tools like Freedom or Cold Turkey can be beneficial, especially if you find yourself frequently checking social media on your laptop.

In extreme cases, if self-discipline is a significant challenge, entrust a family member or friend to change your account passwords. They can provide you with the passwords only after the detox period concludes.

- **Plan What You Will Do During Your Detox**

This step involves preparing for the void left by social media. Plan activities to fill your spare time, replacing the habit of scrolling through your feeds. Consider engaging in non-digital pursuits like reading, spending time with friends and family, learning a new language or skill, working on a side project or business, and incorporating physical activities such as exercising or practicing yoga. Planning and actively engaging in these activities will help you realize how much time social media used to occupy in your day.

If you find yourself with downtime during the detox, use it as an opportunity to meditate or practice mindfulness. For those feeling adventurous, incorporating a meditation retreat into your detox can be a bold and rewarding choice.

- **Replace Digital Habits With Productive Alternatives**

If you find yourself wanting to substitute your digital habits with more productive alternatives, you might want to consider downloading the Kindle app. This allows you to read books during downtime or moments of boredom. You can also explore podcasts or audiobooks, start writing, or take an online course. These activities not only keep you engaged but also contribute to personal growth and development.

By following these steps, you set yourself up for a successful and enriching social media detox, allowing you to rediscover a more balanced and mindful way of living.

It is important to note that a social media detox is a personal journey, and its success hinges on your commitment and mindfulness. Embrace the chance to reconnect with yourself and the world around you, welcoming the positive changes that accompany this intentional break from the digital world.

CULTIVATING GRATITUDE

Practicing gratitude isn't just a pleasant notion; it's a potent tool for enhancing mental health. Cultivating a grateful mindset can yield numerous scientifically proven benefits, contributing to overall well-being. Here are seven such advantages (Martinez, 2023):

- Expressing gratitude is a powerful tool that positively impacts various aspects of your life. It goes beyond good manners and toward fostering new connections and relationships. Studies show that thanking others, whether for a kind gesture or professional assistance, can lead to new opportunities and friendships.
- Gratitude also influences physical health as grateful individuals report fewer aches and pains, maintaining a sense of overall well-being. Those expressing gratitude tend to prioritize health,

engaging in regular exercise and check-ups, potentially contributing to a longer and healthier life.

- On the psychological front, gratitude acts as a potent force in reducing toxic emotions. Research by gratitude expert Robert Emmons highlights its effectiveness in increasing happiness and decreasing feelings of depression, addressing negative emotions like envy and resentment.

- Socially, gratitude enhances interactions by promoting empathy and reducing aggression. Individuals with higher gratitude levels are more likely to exhibit kindness, even when faced with unkind behavior, leading to reduced desires for retaliation.

- Gratitude positively influences sleep quality. Maintaining a gratitude journal and taking just 15 minutes before bedtime to reflect on positive aspects of your life can improve sleep duration and quality.

- Moreover, gratitude extends to self-esteem. In athletes, a 2014 study found that gratitude increased self-esteem, which is crucial for optimal performance. Grateful individuals are less inclined to make social comparisons, which lessens resentment toward those with more success. Rather, they appreciate others' achievements without harming their own self-esteem.

- In challenging times, gratitude plays a crucial role in mental strength and resilience. Studies after significant events, such as the Vietnam War and 9/11, reveal that higher levels of gratitude correlate with lower rates of post-traumatic stress disorder and increased resilience. Recognizing and acknowledging gratitude, even amid adversity, fosters mental strength to navigate difficult circumstances.

Simple Ways to be Grateful Everyday

To cultivate gratitude daily, begin by acknowledging small moments of positivity. Take a few minutes each morning to reflect on aspects of your life you appreciate. Whether it's a supportive friend, a comfortable home, or a beautiful sunrise, recognizing these elements sets a positive tone for the day.

Express gratitude verbally or in writing. Share a heartfelt "thank you" with someone who made a difference, or maintain a gratitude journal to document daily moments of appreciation. This simple act helps reinforce positive emotions and fosters a grateful mindset.

Practice mindfulness, focusing on the present moment. Engage your senses, appreciating the sights, sounds, and sensations around you. Mindful breathing can ground you in the now, promoting gratitude for the gift of each moment.

Set aside time for reflection before bed. Recall three things you're thankful for from the day. This bedtime routine allows you to end your day on a positive note and reinforces a grateful mindset over time.

Lastly, consider volunteering or helping others. Acts of kindness not only contribute to a sense of purpose but also cultivate gratitude as you witness the positive impact on others' lives. Embracing these simple habits can infuse your daily life with a sense of appreciation and gratitude.

Gratitude Journal Prompts

Start your gratitude journaling journey with these prompts:

1. Begin each day by jotting down three things you're grateful for, setting a positive tone for the day ahead.
2. Reflect on the little pleasures that bring happiness to your day, from a warm cup of coffee to a smile from a stranger.
3. Recall moments when others showed kindness to you or when you extended kindness to someone else, appreciating the interconnectedness of humanity.
4. Take note of the natural wonders around you, from the vibrant colors of a sunset to the soothing sound of rain.
5. Reflect on challenges you've overcome and lessons learned, expressing gratitude for the strength and resilience you've gained.
6. Acknowledge the people in your life who support and uplift you, recognizing the importance of their presence.
7. Express gratitude for the opportunities and possibilities that lie ahead, fostering optimism and hope for the future.

INTERACTIVE ELEMENT

Incantations for Inner Calm

In neuro-linguistic programming (NLP), incantations empower you to influence your thoughts and emotions positively. This technique involves verbalizing affirmations aloud, harnessing the power of language to shape your mindset. By repeating statements about taking control of your mind, you can interrupt negative thought patterns and cultivate inner calm. NLP recognizes the profound impact of words on your mental state, making incantations a valuable tool for promoting positive change and combating over-thinking.

Some of these incantations include:

- I am in control of my thoughts, and I am steering away from the chaos of overthinking.
- Each breath I take fills me with calmness and clarity, which dissipates unnecessary thoughts.
- My mind is a sanctuary of peace; I choose tranquility over mental chaos.
- I release the need to overanalyze; my mind is clear, and my thoughts are serene.
- In this moment, I choose to be present and free from the burden of overthinking.
- I am the architect of my thoughts; I construct a foundation of peace and positivity.
- Like a gentle river, my thoughts flow smoothly, avoiding the turbulent currents of overthinking.
- I embrace silence and find solace in the stillness of my mind.
- With each heartbeat, I ground myself in the present, letting go of unnecessary mental clutter.
- I am a master of my mind; I dismiss overthinking and welcome mental serenity.
- Thoughts may come and go, but I choose which ones to entertain, cultivating a mindful existence.

- I break free from the chains of overthinking; my mind is liberated and at peace.
- In the garden of my mind, I plant seeds of positivity, not allowing weeds of overthinking to take root.
- I appreciate the power of simplicity; my mind thrives on clarity and focused tranquility.
- I choose calm over chaos; my thoughts align with serenity, and I navigate the waters of my mind with ease.

Incorporate these incantations into your daily routine, repeating them with sincerity and intention. Consistent practice can help rewire your thought patterns, promoting inner calmness and reducing the grip of overthinking on your mind.

CONCLUSION

Trying to find inner peace can be like hiking through the noise of our own thoughts. This guide, wrapped up in the "think AGAIN" framework, hands you some down-to-earth tools to navigate the twisty trails of your mind and foster a mindset that helps combat overthinking. So, first off, you have to recognize the habit of going over the same thoughts again and again. It's like putting up a "Stop" sign in the middle of your mental freeway. Once you spot those repeat offenders, you're on the road to taking back control of your thoughts.

Next up, let's talk self-talk. Your inner chatter is a big deal—it shapes how you feel and see things. Adjusting your self-talk is about flipping the script to be more positive. It's not just fluffy stuff; real studies back up how positive self-talk can dial down stress and amp up your mental well-being so talk to yourself like you're your own biggest fan.

Then there are these sneaky automatic negative thoughts (ANTs). They crawl into your brain and make problems seem like Godzilla-sized monsters. The trick here is to spot these pests and kick them out. Challenging these negative thoughts is like giving them an eviction notice, which makes room for a more optimistic mindset.

Emotions, our internal messengers, are another big player. Tuning into your emotions means you're listening to what your gut is saying. It's like having your own emotional GPS. Studies say this emotional awareness thing is linked to better mental health and smoother relationships so don't just ignore those feelings; give them a little nod.

During the overthinking chaos, the seemingly simple act of mindful breathing emerges as a powerful anchor. Regular practice not only soothes the mind but also cultivates heightened awareness, effectively disrupting the cycle of obsessive thinking.

The philosophical essence lies in embracing the present moment. Developing a non-attachment mindset releases the grip on the past and relinquishes uncertainties about the future. Mindfulness practices, rooted in ancient wisdom and validated by contemporary studies, guide individuals toward a state of mental clarity and tranquility.

As you stand at the threshold of your own journey toward mental clarity, take the first step today. Embrace the practical steps, integrate them into your daily life, and witness the transformation within. Don't just think about it—start your journey toward inner peace now!

If this transformative guide has provided you with insights or nudged you toward overcoming overthinking, consider sharing your experience with others. Your review could be the catalyst for someone else's journey to mental clarity. If this book has made a difference for you, help someone else find their path by writing a review.

REFERENCES

Accept your negative emotions to reduce them. (n.d.). The Berkeley Well-Being Institute. https://www.berkeleywellbeing.com/accept-your-negative-emotions.html

Almeida-Farrell, G., & LCSW. (n.d.). *Tackling negativity bias and cultivating a growth mindset.* Holistic Wellness Practice. https://www.holisticwellnesspractice.com/hwp-blog/2023/08/26/tackling-negativity-bias-and-cultivating-a-growth-mindset

Andra Chantim. (2020, January 31). *Addicted to social media? Here's the best way to detox.* Good Housekeeping. https://www.goodhousekeeping.com/life/g30681374/social-media-detox-tips/

Anwar, Y. (2022). *Stressed to the max? Deep sleep can rewire the anxious brain.* Berkeley. https://news.berkeley.edu/2019/11/04/deep-sleep-can-rewire-the-anxious-brain

Anxiety, worrying, and overthinking. (2020, May 28). Strategic Psychology. https://strategicpsychology.com.au/anxiety-worrying-and-overthinking

Bartwal, N. (2021, October 21). *Role of self-talk in your life.* Times of India Blog. https://timesofindia.indiatimes.com/readersblog/pausesponder sandinbetween/role-of-self-talk-in-your-life-38483/

Beasley, N. (2018, July 13). *9 visualization techniques for stress reduction.* BetterHelp. https://www.betterhelp.com/advice/stress/9-visualization-techniques-for-stress-reduction/

Becker, J. (2022). *How to live in the moment: 10 tips on being present.* Becoming Minimalist. https://www.becomingminimalist.com/10-tips-to-start-living-in-the-present/

Body scan script (Worksheet). (n.d.). Therapist Aid. https://www.therapistaid.com/therapy-worksheet/body-scan-script

Boyer, A. (2021, August 24). *The difference between thinking deeply and over-thinking.* Introvert Dear. https://introvertdear.com/news/the-difference-between-thinking-deeply-and-overthinking/

Brodsky, S. (2023, February 10). *25 journal prompts for when your self-esteem is at rock bottom.* Wondermind. https://www.wondermind.com/article/self-esteem-journal-prompts/

Broening, J. (n.d.). *Unlocking the power: NLP techniques for visualization mastery*. Quenza. https://quenza.com/blog/knowledge-base/nlp-techniques-for-visualization/

Causes of stress. (2017, November). Mind. https://www.mind.org.uk/information-support/types-of-mental-health-problems/stress/causes-of-stress/

Center, K. C. (2021, October 1). *How to deal with emotional triggers*. Kentucky Counseling Center. https://kentuckycounselingcenter.com/how-to-deal-with-emotional-triggers/

Charles R. Swindoll Quotes (Author of The Grace Awakening). (2020). Goodreads. https://www.goodreads.com/author/quotes/5139.Charles_R_Swindoll

Cleveland Clinic. (2021, January 28). *What is stress? Symptoms, signs & more*. Cleveland Clinic. https://my.clevelandclinic.org/health/articles/11874-stress

Conlon, C. (2014, March 5). *40 simple ways to practice gratitude*. Lifehack. https://www.lifehack.org/articles/communication/40-simple-ways-practice-gratitude.html

Cope, S. (2021, April 1). *18 effective time management strategies & techniques*. Upwork. https://www.upwork.com/resources/time-management-strategies

Cote, C. (2022, March 10). *Growth mindset vs. fixed mindset: What's the difference?* Harvard Business School Online. https://online.hbs.edu/blog/post/growth-mindset-vs-fixed-mindset

Courtney, E. A. (2018, February 5). *21 emotion regulation worksheets & strategies*. Positive Psychology. https://positivepsychology.com/emotion-regulation-worksheets-strategies-dbt-skills/#worksheets-emotion-regulation

Crichton-Stuart , C., & Dias, A. (Ren). (2018, August 1). *9 foods that help reduce anxiety*. Medicalnewstoday.com. https://www.medicalnewstoday.com/articles/322652#_noHeaderPrefixedContent

Cronkleton, E. (2019, April 9). *10 breathing techniques*. Healthline. https://www.healthline.com/health/breathing-exercise

Cuncic, A. (2021, November 10). *How do you live in the present?* Verywell Mind. https://www.verywellmind.com/how-do-you-live-in-the-present-5204439

Deering, S. (2020, February 28). *8 grounding techniques for when you're feeling overwhelmed*. Mental Health Conditions. https://www.talkspace.com/mental-health/conditions/articles/grounding-techniques-anxiety/

Dibdin, E. (2022, January 31). *When childhood trauma leads to anxiety.* Psych Central. https://psychcentral.com/anxiety/the-connection-between-childhood-trauma-and-generalized-anxiety-disorder

Diet and mental health. (2022b, January 25). Mentalhealth. https://www.mentalhealth.org.uk/explore-mental-health/a-z-topics/diet-and-mental-health

Doug. (2020, July 20). *8 keys to accepting things that are out of your control.* Foundations Counseling. https://www.yournewfoundation.com/8-keys-to-accepting-things-that-are-out-of-your-control/

Dweck, C. S. (2006). *Mindset: The new psychology of success.* Amazon. My Book

Eckhart Tolle Quotes (Author of The Power of Now). (n.d.). Goodreads. https://www.goodreads.com/author/quotes/4493.Eckhart_Tolle

Elizabeth Scott. (2022, May 23). *What are the main causes of stress?* Verywell Mind. https://www.verywellmind.com/what-are-the-main-causes-of-stress-3145063

Elkhuizen, B. (2023). *The 10 most important benefits of time management.* Bakkerel Khuizen. https://www.bakkerelkhuizen.com/knowledge/the-10-most-important-benefits-of-time-management/?country=I&lang=EN

Emmons, R. (2010, November 17). *10 ways to become more grateful.* Greater Good. https://greatergood.berkeley.edu/article/item/ten_ways_to_become_more_grateful1

Erika. (2020, July 30). *7 best exercises for anxiety and depression.* Talking Circles Therapy & Wellness, LLC. https://talkingcirclestherapy.com/7-best-exercises-for-anxiety-and-depression/

Exercise: The overthinking test. (n.d.). https://overcoming.co.uk/_data/site/148/product/1517/TheOverthinkingTestp.107.pdf

Fargo, S. (2019, November 15). *8 meditation scripts for stress.* Mindfulness Exercises. https://mindfulnessexercises.com/meditation-scripts-for-stress/

Felman, A. (2021, March 23). *What causes anxiety? Environmental factors, genetics, and more.* Medical News Today. https://www.medicalnewstoday.com/articles/323456#environmental-factors

Felton, K. (2020, June 1). *3 workouts to do if you're feeling anxious or depressed.* Health. https://www.health.com/condition/depression/these-are-the-best-exercises-for-anxiety-and-depression

Ferguson, S. (2016, May 17). *What does tolerating uncertainty mean and how can you learn it?* Psych Central. https://psychcentral.com/anxiety/tips-on-tolerating-uncertainty#how-to-tolerate-uncertainty

5 mental benefits of exercise. (2019, May 16). Walden University. https://www.waldenu.edu/online-bachelors-programs/bs-in-psychology/resource/five-mental-benefits-of-exercise

5 tools for making better decisions. (2021, September 17). 42courses. https://www.42courses.com/blog/home/2021/9/17/5-tools-for-making-better-decisions

Flaxington, B. D. (2020, February 4). *The destructive nature of negative self-talk.* Psychology Today. https://www.psychologytoday.com/us/blog/understand-other-people/202002/the-destructive-nature-negative-self-talk

Fox, M. (n.d.). *8 reasons why you should unplug one day a week.* Forbes. https://www.forbes.com/sites/meimeifox/2019/09/24/8-reasons-why-you-should-unplug-one-day-a-week/?sh=59f6ce541b79

Guided imagery scripts: Free relaxation scripts. (n.d.). Inner Health Studio. https://www.innerhealthstudio.com/guided-imagery-scripts.html

Gupta, A. (2022, April 29). *Are you stuck in the vicious cycle of overthinking? It's risky, warns an expert.* Healthshots. https://www.healthshots.com/mind/mental-health/heres-how-overthinking-can-impact-your-overall-health/

How does overthinking impact our decision-making power? (2023, September 14). Psychologs Magazine | Mental Health Magazine | Psychology Magazine | Self-Help Magazine. https://www.psychologs.com/how-does-overthinking-impact-our-decision-making-power/

How to deal with uncertainty. (n.d.). Real Simple. https://www.realsimple.com/work-life/life-strategies/cope-uncertainty

How to reduce stress through mindfulness | Rehabilitation Research and Training Center on Aging With Physical Disabilities. (n.d.). Agerrtc. https://agerrtc.washington.edu/info/factsheets/mindfulness#techniques

How to use mental anchoring to reduce anxiety. (2017). BoomBoom. https://boomboomnaturals.com/blogs/news/how-to-use-mental-anchoring-to-reduce-anxiety

Ivan Nuru quotes (Author of Offering My Heart). (n.d.). Goodreads. https://www.goodreads.com/author/quotes/17199757.Ivan_Nuru

Jenks, M. (2020, September 17). *How neutral self-talk can radically change your life.* The Edge. https://www.elonedge.com/blog/2020/9/17/how-neutral-self-talk-can-radically-change-your-life

Karimova, H. (2017, December 24). *The emotion wheel: What it is and how to use it.* Positive Psychology. https://positivepsychology.com/emotion-wheel/

Kim. (2011, May 5). *NLP reframing, finding the right spin.* NLP Mentor. https://nlp-mentor.com/nlp-reframing/

Klynn, B. (2021, June 22). *Emotional regulation: Skills, exercises, and strategies.* BetterUp. https://www.betterup.com/blog/emotional-regulation-skills

Kristenson, S. (2021, December 12). *31 affirmations for positive thinking that will change your life.* Happier Human. https://www.happierhuman.com/affirmations-positive-thinking/

Lidia Longorio Quote: "Don't believe everything you tell yourself." (n.d.). Quotefancy. https://quotefancy.com/quote/3331773/Lidia-Longorio-Don-t-believe-everything-you-tell-yourself

Lindberg, S. (2023, March 23). *How your environment affects your mental health.* Verywell Mind. https://www.verywellmind.com/how-your-environment-affects-your-mental-health-5093687

Martinez, J. N. (2023, January 25). *7 scientifically proven benefits of gratitude.* LinkedIn. https://www.linkedin.com/pulse/7-scientifically-proven-benefits-gratitude-joseph-n-martinez

Mastering Socratic questioning (Guide). (n.d.). Therapist Aid. https://www.therapistaid.com/therapy-guide/mastering-socratic-questioning

Mawer, R. (2020, February 28). *17 proven tips to sleep better at night.* Healthline. https://www.healthline.com/nutrition/17-tips-to-sleep-better

Max Depree Famous quote: "We cannot become what we want by remaining what we are." (n.d.). Treasure quotes. https://www.treasurequotes.com/quotes/we-cannot-become-what-we-want-by-remaining-wha

Mayo Clinic Staff. (2017). *Forgiveness: Letting go of grudges and bitterness.* Mayo Clinic. https://www.mayoclinic.org/healthy-lifestyle/adult-health/in-depth/forgiveness/art-20047692

McAdam, E. (2023, November 8). *Automatic negative thoughts—Therapy in a Nutshell.* Therapy in a Nutshell. https://therapyinanutshell.com/automatic-negative-thoughts/

Meaghan, R. (2022, June 21). *How to use meditation for stress.* Talk Space. https://www.talkspace.com/blog/meditation-for-stress/

Meek, W. (2008, July 27). *How to improve self-esteem with generalized anxiety disorder.* Verywell Mind; Verywellmind. https://www.verywellmind.com/anxiety-and-self-esteem-1393168

Moeller Gorman, R. (2020, March 16). *7 tricks to tame your mind and stop overthinking just about everything, finally.* Shape. https://www.shape.com/lifestyle/mind-and-body/stress-overthinking

Morin, A. (2017, June 25). *9 signs you're a perfectionist (and that's not a good thing)*. Forbes. https://www.forbes.com/sites/amymorin/2017/06/25/9-signs-youre-a-perfectionist-and-thats-not-a-good-thing/?sh=482f2dbf5ca3

Nature: How connecting with nature benefits our mental health. (2022). Mentalhealth. https://www.mentalhealth.org.uk/our-work/research/nature-how-connecting-nature-benefits-our-mental-health

Nature therapy: The benefits of nature for mental health. (2021, April 22). Kentucky Counseling Center. https://kentuckycounselingcenter.com/benefits-of-nature-to-the-mental-health/

Nunez, K. (2020, August 10). *The benefits of progressive muscle relaxation and how to do it*. Healthline. https://www.healthline.com/health/progressive-muscle-relaxation

Our brain's negative bias. (2016). Psychology Today. https://www.psychologytoday.com/us/articles/200306/our-brains-negative-bias

Overthinking disorder: Is it a mental illness? (2022, May 16). Cleveland Clinic. https://health.clevelandclinic.org/is-overthinking-a-mental-illness

Pietrangeli, K. (2014, January 17). *Think before reacting: How to use your mental pause button*. Tiny Buddha. https://tinybuddha.com/blog/think-before-reacting-use-mental-pause-button/

Progressive muscle relaxation script. (n.d.). https://www.therapistaid.com/worksheets/progressive-muscle-relaxation-script

A quote by Atticus. (n.d.). Goodreads. https://www.goodreads.com/quotes/11617937-we-drink-the-poison-our-minds-pour-for-us-and

A quote by Henry Ford. (2019). Goodreads. https://www.goodreads.com/quotes/978-whether-you-think-you-can-or-you-think-you-can-t--you-re

A quote by Hermann Hesse. (n.d.). Goodreads. https://www.goodreads.com/quotes/7540208-within-you-there-is-a-stillness-and-a-sanctuary-to

A quote from Fall With Me. (n.d.). Goodreads https://www.goodreads.com/quotes/8101103-sometimes-when-things-are-falling-apart-they-may-actually-be

Raypole, C. (2019, May 24). *Grounding techniques: 30 techniques for anxiety, PTSD, and more*. Healthline. https://www.healthline.com/health/grounding-techniques#physical-techniques

Raypole, C. (2020, March 26). *Body scan meditation: Benefits and how to do it*. Healthline. https://www.healthline.com/health/body-scan-meditation

Robinson, L., Segal, J., & Smith, M. (2023, February 28). *The mental health*

benefits of exercise. Help Guide. https://www.helpguide.org/articles/
healthy-living/the-mental-health-benefits-of-exercise.htm

Roncero, A. (2021, June 21). *Automatic thoughts: How you can identify and fix
them*. Betterup. https://www.betterup.com/blog/automatic-thoughts

Rosen, D. A. (2019, April 17). *The connection between diet and mental health*.
Center for Treatment of Anxiety & Mood Disorders. https://www.
centerforanxietydisorders.com/diet-and-mental-health/

Schenck, L. K. (2011, June 18). *Recognize your emotions in 6 steps*. Mindfulness Muse. https://www.mindfulnessmuse.com/dialectical-behavior-
therapy/recognize-your-emotions-in-6-steps

Segal, J., Smith, M., Robinson, L., & Segal, R. (2023, April 5). *Stress symptoms,
signs, and causes: Improving your ability to handle stress*. Helpguide. https://
www.helpguide.org/articles/stress/stress-symptoms-signs-and-
causes.htm

7 yoga poses that relieve stress and anxiety. (n.d.). Select Health. https://
selecthealth.org/blog/2022/06/yoga-poses

Seven-signs-you-are-too-much-of-a-perfectionist. (n.d.). Walden. https://www.
waldenu.edu/online-masters-programs/ms-in-psychology/resource/
seven-signs-you-are-too-much-of-a-perfectionist

Should adults reduce their screen time? (2018, February 14). Scripps Health.
https://www.scripps.org/news_items/6310-8-tips-to-reduce-screen-
time-for-adults

Simple ways to spend more time in nature. (n.d.). Extension. https://extension.
usu.edu/mentalhealth/articles/simple-ways-to-spend-more-time-in-
nature

Sivakumar, S. (2023, December 21). *Anchoring in NLP: Understanding its
types, benefits, and a script*. Emo Care. https://emocare.co.in/anchoring-
in-nlp-understanding-its-types-benefits-and-a-script/

16 best ways to reduce screen time. (2022, September 14). Home of Internet
Privacy. https://www.expressvpn.com/blog/ways-to-reduce-or-limit-
your-screen-time/

Sparks, D. (2019, May 29). *Mayo mindfulness: overcoming negative self-talk*.
News Network. https://newsnetwork.mayoclinic.org/discussion/
mayo-mindfulness-overcoming-negative-self-talk/

Stein, D. (2015, January 5). *Why you worry: Obsessing, overthinking, and over-
analyzing explained*. https://effectivetherapysolutions.com/anxiety/why-
you-worry-obsessing-overthinking-and-overanalyzing-explained

Stop worrying... or at least postpone it. (2014, April 20). Cognitive Behavioral

Therapy Los Angeles. https://cogbtherapy.com/cbt-blog/2014/4/20/stop-worrying-or-at-least-postpone-it

Straw, E. (2023, November 10). *Focus only on what's in your control*. Success Starts Within. https://www.successstartswithin.com/blog/importance-of-focusing-on-whats-in-your-control

Sutton, J. (2021, December 20). *7 stress-relief breathing exercises for calming your mind*. Positive Psychology. https://positivepsychology.com/breathing-exercises-for-stress-relief/

Tanasugarn, A. (2023, September 5). *Are you in a pattern of overthinking?* Psychology Today. https://www.psychologytoday.com/intl/blog/understanding-ptsd/202309/are-you-in-a-pattern-of-overthinking

Temple, E. (2023, March 31). *Overthinking and perfectionism*. Critical Fallibilism. https://criticalfallibilism.com/overthinking-and-perfectionism/

10 popular time management techniques. (n.d.). Bright pod. https://www.brightpod.com/boost/10-popular-time-management-techniques

10 ways to overcome perfectionism. (2021, April 15). Oregon Counseling. https://oregoncounseling.com/article/10-ways-to-overcome-perfectionism/

The cost of overthinking: Why it's time to stop worrying about the future. (n.d.). Linkedin. https://www.linkedin.com/pulse/cost-overthinking-why-its-time-stop-worrying-future-gary-miles

The power of neutral affirmations. (2020, July 10). Urban Balance. https://www.urbanbalance.com/the-power-of-neutral-affirmations/

The six step reframe technique. (2011, May 6). NLP Mentor. https://nlp-mentor.com/six-step-reframe/

3 side effects of overthinking. (2020, January 3). PharmEasy Blog. https://pharmeasy.in/blog/overthinking-to-what-extent-can-it-damage-your-life/

Top 10 tips for... developing a positive growth mindset. (n.d.). CHRysos HR Solutions Limited. https://www.chrysos.org.uk/blog/top-10-tips-for-developing-a-positive-growth-mind

12 ways to make better decisions. (n.d.). Indeed Career Guide. https://www.indeed.com/career-advice/career-development/how-to-make-better-decisions

Using ABC Please to manage overwhelming emotions with DBT. (n.d.). Grouport therapy. https://www.grouporttherapy.com/blog/abc-please-dbt

Wahome, C. (2021, August 24). *How to overcome perfectionism*. WebMD. https://www.webmd.com/balance/features/how-to-overcome-perfectionism

Walker, S. (2022a, April 6). *100 negative self talk examples to stop now.* Empowered and Thriving. https://empoweredandthriving.com/nega tive-self-talk-examples/

Walker, S. (2022b, April 6). *100 positive self talk examples to adopt now.* Empowered and Thriving. https://empoweredandthriving.com/posi tive-self-talk-examples/

Waters, S. (2021, June 9). *The power of positive self talk (and how you can use it).* Betterup. https://www.betterup.com/blog/self-talk

What is a growth mindset and how can you develop one? (2022, April 25). Future Learn. https://www.futurelearn.com/info/blog/general/develop-growth-mindset

What is a growth mindset? 8 steps to develop one. (2019, April 12). Western Governors University. https://www.wgu.edu/blog/what-is-growth-mindset-8-steps-develop-one1904.html#:~:

Williams, R. (2018, July 16). *Are we "Hardwired" to think and feel negatively?* Ray Williams. https://raywilliams.ca/are-we-hardwired-to-think-and-feel-negatively/

Witmer, S. A. (2023, March 24). *What is overthinking, and how do I stop over-thinking everything?* GoodRx. https://www.goodrx.com/health-topic/mental-health/how-can-i-stop-overthinking-everything

Made in the USA
Las Vegas, NV
21 November 2024

12189137R00121